The Psalter

In rhyming verse

by

TJW Thornes

WASH HOUSE PUBLISHING

Poetry

Published by Wash House Publishing 2021

Printed on demand by CPI Group.
The CPI Group is committed to the prevention of pollution and continual improvement to reduce our effect on the environment.

Copyright © Tobias Thornes, 2021.

ISBN 978-1-3999-0272-4

All Rights Reserved. All or part of this publication may be reproduced, reprinted or otherwise disseminated only when accompanied by acknowledgement of the author.

For your God and mine.

Let my words, my meditations deep,
Be good and right,
Be found to be acceptable
And precious in your sight.

— Psalm 119

Contents

Foreword	7		
Psalm: 1	8	Psalm: 29	74
2	10	30	76
3	12	31	78
4	14	32	82
5	16	33	84
6	18	34	87
7	20	35	89
8	23	36	94
9	24	37	96
10	27	38	99
11	30	39	102
12	32	40	104
13	34	41	107
14	36	42	109
15	38	43	110
16	40	44	111
17	42	45	114
18	45	46	116
19	51	47	118
20	54	48	120
21	56	49	122
22	58	50	125
23	60	51	129
24	62	52	132
25	64	53	134
26	67	54	136
27	69	55	137
28	72	56	140

Psalm:	57	142	Psalm:	88	225
	58	144		89	227
	59	146		90	236
	60	149		91	238
	61	151		92	240
	62	153		93	242
	63	156		94	243
	64	158		95	247
	65	160		96	249
	66	162		97	251
	67	165		98	253
	68	166		99	255
	69	172		100	257
	70	177		101	258
	71	178		102	260
	72	181		103	264
	73	183		104	267
	74	186		105	272
	75	189		106	278
	76	191		107	286
	77	193		108	291
	78	196		109	294
	79	206		110	300
	80	208		111	302
	81	210		112	304
	82	213		113	306
	83	215		114	308
	84	218		115	309
	85	220		116	311
	86	222		117	314
	87	224		118	315

Psalm: 119	i	319	Psalm: 125	352
	ii	320	126	353
	iii	321	127	354
	iv	322	128	355
	v	323	129	356
	vi	325	130	357
	vii	326	131	358
	viii	327	132	359
	ix	328	133	361
	x	329	134	362
	xi	330	135	363
	xii	332	136	366
	xiii	333	137	368
	xiv	334	138	370
	xv	335	139	372
	xvi	336	140	376
	xvii	337	141	378
	xviii	339	142	380
	xix	340	143	382
	xx	341	144	384
	xxi	342	145	386
	xxii	343	146	390
120		345	147	392
121		346	148	395
122		348	149	397
123		350	150	399
124		351		

Foreword

For thousands of years the Psalms have been at the heart of theistic worship, originally as songs sung by the ancient Jewish people whose history the Old Testament records. Many of the 150 Psalms are ascribed to King David; others' origins are unknown, and their subject matter hints at a later date. Their words may have brought comfort and hope to a people that ended up in exile, far from home.

Christians, too, have found in the Psalms both wonder and wisdom, containing as they do the whole spectrum of human emotion. In the Psalms you will find sorrow and anguish, joy and praise, homesickness, loneliness, dejection and thanksgiving. There is a psalm for every occasion, and it is little wonder that they are said or sung, as part of public services or alone, every day by Christians of many denominations.

My aim of writing this book of 'psalm poems' is not to replace existing translations of the psalms into English, many of which very powerfully evoke the sentiments of the original authors so many centuries ago. Rather, I hope that translating the Psalms into rhyming verse – whilst trying to keep as much of the meaning as possible – may allow them to be read through a fresh perspective that regains some of the musical rhythm otherwise lost in translation. I do hope that you will find the resulting verses enjoyable to dip into from time to time.

T J W Thornes
16th August 2021

1

Blessed be all they
Who have not walked in wicked ways,
Nor sat among the scornful,
Nor slipped in sin as strays,
Nor lingered where is evil:
The Lord's law is their delight,
Who meditate upon His goodly word
Both day and night.

Like a tree beside swift streams
They drink of waters fresh,
With leaves that do not wither
And rich fruit of goodly flesh;
Whatever they endeavour it will prosper –
All they do –
But O, accursed wicked one,
It is not so with you.

You will soon be swept away
Like chaff blown on the wind,
You will never enter with the righteous:
You have sinned.
When the day of judgement comes,
You'll quake and fall down flat:
So for all the wicked,
Who in easy pride once sat.

The Lord, He knows the righteous way
    Wherein the godly walk,
But everlasting death lies down
    The road the wicked stalk.

2

Why do nations war and strive,
The peoples pout and plot?
In vain they scheme together
To attempt what they ought not:
The rulers of the Earth rise up,
Together they consult.
With wicked whispers they conspire;
The Lord they put at fault.

'We'll break his bonds asunder,
We shall cast away his cords!'
But God will laugh to scorn those imps
Who set themselves as lords.
High heaven will deride them,
And in fury God will fume –
His righteous wrath will eat them up,
His terror will consume.

'I have set in state my King
Upon my holy hill –
He, through whom these wicked men
Will taste a bitter pill.
You, my son, I have begotten
And ordained to rule;
Ask of me and I will put
The nations 'neath your stool.

'All the ends of Earth are yours;
You'll break them with your rod,
And smash them like a potter's vessel
Over which you've trod.'
Be wise, then, kings and mark my words,
You judges of the Earth –
Serve the Lord and fear Him
Who alone can give you worth,

Lest he push you off your seat
In anger at your sin
And you fall and perish
On the way you travel in.
For His wrath is kindled quick,
As dry brush catches fire;
But happy he who trusts in God
And does not know His ire.

3

O God, how many cruel foes
Have set themselves on me!
Many rise to swallow,
Like a great tempestuous sea!
To my soul their words wound deep:
'There is no help for you –
You trust in what? A worthless God?
What good can he do you?'

But you, O Lord, my mighty shield,
You will my frame surround
And lift my head above all these
Who in such sin abound.
You, God, are my glory,
And to you I cry aloud;
You, I know, will answer me
And wrap me in your shroud.

Every day I rise again,
Each night in sleep I lie,
Because by your sweet sustenance
I live and do not die.
I will never be afraid,
Though hordes and droves attack:
They set themselves against me
But my God will drive them back.

Rise up, O Lord, deliver me
And break their wicked teeth;
Strike my foes upon the cheek
And thrust them from beneath.
You are our salvation, Lord:
Our life belongs to you;
May your lasting blessing
Rest upon your faithful few.

4

Answer me, O God, of righteousness –
I call to thee,
You who midst the jaws of trouble
Won my liberty.
Have mercy now upon me, God,
And hear my pleaful prayer;
Look upon the wicked ones
And see their sinful snare!

How long will you vain nobles
Venture to dishonour me?
How long will you with false pursuits
Infatuated be?
The Lord has shown His love to me,
His way He has made clear:
When I call upon my God
I know that He will hear.

Stand now still, in awe of Him,
And cease your strife of sin;
Commune with your own heart
And seek His wisdom from within:
Lie upon your bed, be still,
And listen to the Lord:
The sacrifice of righteousness
Is one you can afford.

There is One that you may trust:
But God, and God alone.
Follow not the many who say,
'Where is goodness known?'
Be you sure, it is the Lord
Who sets injustice right:
It is He who into darkness
Shines His stunning light,
Pouring from His shining face,
And straight into my heart,
The gladness of a thousand suns
And brighter to impart!

More than any corn or wine
Or oil could satisfy:
God will give contentment
When at last to rest I lie,
Down upon my weary bed,
Where I shall sleep in peace,
For God alone will keep me safe
And all my fears release.

5

Listen, Lord, to my lament –
O hearken to my voice,
And hear the cry of one who calls
To you, my only choice,

My God and King – for in the morning
You will hear my prayer,
When in dark hours before the dawn
Unto the skies I stare,

Making mine appeal to you
And waiting for your light
To break upon the darkness
That cannot endure your sight.

You take no glee in wickedness,
No evil dwells with you;
The boastful fall before your face
And wicked schemers too;

You stamp out those who deal in lies,
The bloodthirsty abhor:
Those who love deceit will find
Destruction laid in store.

Lead me in your righteous ways:
Lord, save me from their deeds;
No truthful words trip from their tongues,
Their heart injustice breeds;

Their throat is like a sepulchre,
Their breath by boasts made foul:
They flatter with the tongue of death
And hollow is their howl.

Punish them, O God:
Destroy them by their own device.
They set it as a snare for me,
So let it be their price.

They as rebels rise against you –
Cast these sinners out,
But as for me, in your straight ways
I walk, and do not doubt.

I will come into your house
And bow before your seat;
By your precious mercy you
Will thither lead my feet.

All who seek your refuge
Will find shelter and be glad,
And we shall sing for ever where
We never shall be sad.

You, Lord, are our blessings' source,
Our shield and defence,
And those who love your name shall lead
Your exultation hence.

6

O Lord, let me not feel the fury
Of your anger's fire:
Chasten not this broken wretch,
Rebuke me not in ire!

Have mercy on me, Lord,
For I am sorely scarred and weak;
My bones are stretched and buckled
And your healing touch I seek.

My soul shakes with the terror
Of the things that I have seen;
How long will you turn away
In wrath at what I've been?

Turn again – deliver me,
For mercy's sake please save
My soul – for who can thank you
From the silence of the grave?

In death you are forgotten:
Let not darkness be my fate;
Weary with my groaning,
All my wasted days I wait.

By night I drench my pillow,
For my face, it floods with tears;
Mine eyes are blind with crying,
Worn away by sobs of years,

Because of all mine enemies
Who mock on every side –
Depart from me, you wicked ones,
For God will not abide

The evil of your doings!
Now my God has heard my plea,
He has listened to my voice,
And He will rescue me.

All my foes will be confused
And thwarted at their game;
All who sought to mock me
Will at once turn back in shame.

7

God, my God, I hide in you,
My refuge from pursuit:
In your strength, deliver me
From those who seek my life!
They long to maul me as a lion,
To beat me like a brute,
And there is none to save me
From the arrow and the knife!

God, if I have done these things
That, lying, they allege;
If any stain of wickedness
Upon my hands you find;
If I with evil deeds repaid my friend,
Or broke my pledge,
Or with no aggravation plundered
Enemies of mine,

Then let them overtake me,
Tear my life with tooth and claw;
Let them charge and trample me
To nothing on the ground;
Let my honour fall from me,
Forgotten on the floor –
But God, you know in righteousness
My judgement has been sound.

Rise up in your fiery wrath;
Against their fury break
And lift yourself against them
For the justice you command:
Let the proud assembly
Of the peoples now awake
And judge me –
For these baseless accusations will not stand.

Be seated high, and speak your judgement:
Innocent I am;
Establish us, the righteous
Whose heart, mind and soul you test.
Surely, they provoke your anger
With their wicked sham:
Let the malice of the evil
Now be brought to rest.

God, you are my lasting shield –
You save the true of heart,
But whet your sword in judgement
On all those who won't repent:
Weapons of destruction you have crafted,
In your art;
Against the evil, your great bow
Have fiery arrows bent.

See, they labour on their lies:
Pregnant with their plots,
They conceive with seeds of evil,
Give birth to deceit;
All day long they dig deep pits
That others may be got,
But they will trip and fall themselves
When you force their retreat.

They will flee and fall
Into the holes they dug so well;
The mischief of their minds
Upon their own heads now rebounds:
In violence they sought to bring
On others living hell,
But I will thank and sing to God –
In goodness He abounds!

8

O God, you are our governor: how glorious your name!
The highest heavens praise you,
and the youngest babes the same,
For all the universe is yours, your fingers' work of love:
You set the stars and hung the Moon
high in the heaven above.

When I consider all this work, and your almighty plan,
It strikes me with amazement you consider meagre man:
A mere mortal, born to mortal parents on the Earth –
Yet you place him just beneath the angels from his birth,

Crowning him with glory
and the honour that's your due,
Giving him dominion over what belongs to you:

All the sheep and oxen have you trusted to his hand,
Even wild beasts and birds obeying his command,
And whatsoever moves among the deep paths of the sea.
How can all this splendour be entrusted, Lord, to me?

O God, you are a stronghold,
and you still the troubled waves;
Your foes will not prevail against the One
who gives and saves.

O God, be thou my governor, my lowly steps uplift,
That I may be made worthy to receive this priceless gift!

9

With my whole heart, God, I thank you
For the deeds you've done,
For the marvellous works you've wrought,
The victory you've won.

Making music to your name, rejoicing,
I'll be glad,
For you have heard my humble cause,
The troubles I have had.

Mine enemies, you drove them back –
They stumbled and fell down,
When you in righteous judgement
On your throne sat in renown

To rebuke the nations
And have wicked men brought low,
To blot their names out of your book
And punishment bestow.

The enemy assaulted me;
You laid your city waste,
You vindicate the righteous
While the false your fury taste.

You will rule for ever
While the wicked are forgot,
You will rule with righteousness
And share out equal lot.

In times of trouble you will be
The saviour of the pressed,
You who never fail the ones
Who in your refuge rest.

Zion, sing the praises
Of the Lord who dwells in you;
Dare among the peoples
To declare what He will do!

He avenged the blood of those
Who by oppression fell;
He will not forget me
But will save my life as well.

Have mercy on me, Lord:
O lift me up from death's dark gate,
Consider how I suffer trouble
At the hands of hate.

The nations dug a pit for me;
Into it will they trip
And fall into the snare they set
And hoped my foot to grip.

The Lord is known by acts of justice,
Fair are His commands;
Hence the wicked sink
Through the foul works of their own hands.

Down into the land of darkness –
Thither do they go,
All who don't remember God,
Nor any reverence show.

Arise now, Lord –
The time has come to let them feel your fear,
That the nations on
Their own mortality may peer

And see that mere mortal men
Have not the upper hand,
But the poor and needy
Through their trust in you shall stand.

10

When trouble comes upon us, Lord,
Why stand so far away?
Why hide yourself and help us not
Upon the dreadful day?

The wicked powers strut their pride
And persecute the poor;
They boast of what they want themselves
And your name they ignore.

Let their crafty schemes come back
And catch them unaware –
Covetous, to curse
And to revile the Lord they dare!

In their arrogance they set
At nought God's power to save;
'Who is God to take revenge
On what we do?' they rave.

Set in ways of wickedness,
Your judgements they fling off:
They do not know your justice,
At opponents they but scoff.

In their sinful hearts they whisper,
'I shall never fall:
No obstacle shall stop me,
No calamity befall.'

With their mouth they lie and curse,
Their kindly words a fraud:
Cruelly they manipulate,
With mischief they reward.

They lurk down darkened alleyways,
The innocent they slay,
Watching for the helpless poor
To tread that fateful way.

As a lion waits to pounce,
They spy upon the poor
And feast on desperate victims
Which into the net they draw;

Sucking up their blood like spiders
Feasting on mere mites:
People break and crumple
Once they set them in their sights.

As they gobble unjust gains
They say, 'God doesn't see –
He forgets, He hides His face,
He'll never hamper me.'

Rise and lift your hand, O Lord,
And push these wicked down:
Do not leave the humble poor
In webs of woe to drown!

Why should evil people say
That you will not avenge?
They speak so scornfully of you –
Why take you not revenge?

You must see our misery,
So take it in your hand:
Let the orphans trust themselves
To you, and reprimand

The wicked who oppress them,
Malicious to the heart –
Search their every evil out,
Their every rotten part!

You shall reign for ever,
Though the nations rise and fall;
You will hear the people's plea
And heed the poor man's call –

You will show them favour
When they pour out all their grief,
And grant the helpless and oppressed
Salvation and relief.

You will break the wicked,
Thrust the sceptre from their hand:
No more will our people flee
In terror from their land.

11

I took the Lord to be my refuge –
Now I need not fear;
I'll not flee into the hills
When enemies appear.

'The wicked bend their bow', you say,
'To strike their arrows deep,
To shoot at all the righteous
From the shadows where they creep!

'Flee away and save yourself!'
You shout as if distraught,
'They've shattered our foundations,
All the good are come to naught!'

Do you not recall?
It is the Lord who sits on high,
In His holy Temple,
On His throne above the sky.

He beholds their wickedness,
He judges mortal men –
The righteous and the wicked,
They will not escape His plan.

He will rain down coals of fire
And sulphur on the head
Of every one who shuns Him
And loves violence instead.

Pain shall be their portion,
Scorching wind shall be their drink –
Under their own sins
Will every cruel tyrant sink.

For the Lord is righteous,
He delights in righteous deeds;
To loving folk He shows His face
And plenteous manna feeds.

12

I call on you to help me, Lord:
None other now remains
Of those who once were godly:
All the human race are strayed.
Faithfulness has vanished:
Not a single one refrains
From falsehood, as each neighbour
By their neighbours is betrayed.

They flatter with their lying lips
But speak from double hearts –
If only God would shut for good
Their vomit-spewing throats!
If only He would cut the tongues
That twist with wicked arts,
Who proudly say, 'we will prevail'
And glory in their boasts.

'Our lips will win us honour –
Who will lord it over us?'
But God who sits above them
Sees the groaning of the poor,
The oppressed and needy,
All the hurt that evil does:
'I will rise and set them
In the safety they long for.'

Lord, your words are pure words:
Smooth as silver set by fire,
And purified seven times,
They shimmer so with truth.
Guard us from this generation, God,
Whose deeds are dire:
Hide us from their wickedness
Beneath your mercy's roof.

The wicked strut on every side,
Devoid of love and grace,
When what is vile is vaunted
By this crooked human race!

13

How long shall I languish here
In waiting for you, Lord?
How long will you forget me,
And hide your face away?
How long will blades of anguish
Slice my poor soul like a sword,
And grief well up within my heart
To drown me, day by day?

Will you let mine enemy
In triumph stand and mock?
Will you let mine eyes be darkened,
As I sleep in death?
Will you not look on and see,
And answer me, my rock,
Before my foes, rejoicing,
Utter curses with each breath?

They will say in slander,
'See – against him I prevail!'
They will think me fallen,
If you come not to mine aid.
I have put my trust in you –
Your love will never fail –
And I know I shall rejoice
When in your arms I'm laid.

I will rest in safety
In the shadow of your wings:
A shadow not of darkness
But protection from the snare;
I will pour out songs of joy,
Just as the sweet bird sings,
To you, O God, for you
Have held be generously there.

14

It's a fool who ways within his heart,
'There is no God',
Who walks about in wickedness
And wields oppression's rod,
Who dabbles in corruption –
For not one of them does good –
While God looks down and sees
His children have not understood.

There is none with wisdom:
No one seeks to know His will;
All alike have fallen to temptation,
Doing ill.
None there are with knowledge,
All in evil deeds delight,
Who give no thought to God –
Abominations in His sight!

They eat up goodly people
Just as though they munched on bread,
But they shall fall into great fear,
Shall quickly quake instead:
Be ye sure, the righteous,
They have God upon their side,
But those who would confound the poor
Our God will not abide.

He will be their refuge:
All the ill-abused and weak,
So let Israel set a watch,
Their coming Lord to seek!
He will raise their fortunes,
He will lift them from the dust,
And gird them all with gladness
Who in Israel's saviour trust.

15

Who may share with you, O God,
  The shelter of your tent?
Who may rest in happiness
  Upon your holy hill?
Those who to corruption
Have their earthly lives not bent,
Those who practise what is right
  And bring about your will,

Who testify to truthful things
  With all their mind and heart,
Who do not twist their tongues to utter
  Verses of deceit,
Who to their friend and neighbour do
  No evil deeds impart,
Who do not pour out scorn
To make their neighbours' woes complete.

In their sight the wicked, though he boast,
  Has no esteem –
The people whom they honour are
  The rich in love of God;
They do not give false promises
  While in their heart they scheme,
Nor take a bribe and see the guiltless
  Punished with the rod.

They do not lend to friend or stranger
Asking for returns,
Nor hope to heap up wealth
Exacting interest from the poor:
Whoever does these things for love of God
His payment earns,
For they shall never fall
But dwell with Him for evermore.

16

I hide in you, my God –
O please preserve me from my woe!
I give my life to you, my Lord
On whom my good depends.
I delight in noble hearts,
Who in your good ways go;
Those serving their invented idols,
They are not my friends.

Legions of those lurid no-gods
Fill their houses up;
Their blasphemous blind offerings
I shirk, nor speak their names.
For the Lord himself,
He is my portion and my cup:
From your hands falls my fortune,
Which their fickle riches shames.

My share falls in the fairest land,
A portion that will last,
And I will bless the Lord
Who all my wisdom does impart;
I have set the Lord beside me,
He will hold me fast,
Nor suffer me to stumble,
Who by night instructs my heart.

For this cause I sing for joy:
My soul with gladness wells,
My body too in safety rests
While I abide in Earth,
For God will not abandon me
When toll my deathly bells:
His presence is the path of life,
And everlasting mirth.

17

Hear my cause, O God:
Consider well my just complaint;
Heed my honest pleading,
For no lies my lips will taint.
Send my vindication,
For you know that I do right:
Weigh my heart's intentions
And my secret thoughts by night.

Refine me, search me, try me –
You will find that I am pure;
I speak no deceit
That I might worldly wealth procure:
I hang upon your goodly words,
I follow your command;
I stumble not, for on your paths
My feet securely stand.

I call on you, O God,
For lo I know you will respond:
Incline thine ear and hear me,
Rescue me from my despond!
Show me loving-kindness,
Mercy marvellous renew,
O saviour of all those
Who, seeking refuge, flee to you.

Keep me, as an apple
Ever pleasant to your eye;
Hide me, in the shadow
Of your wings while dangers fly –
When the wicked shoot their arrows,
Seeking for my life,
When my foes assault me
And most bitter is my strife.

They will show no pity,
They have closed their icy heart;
And their mouths but boasting lies
And wicked words impart.
Surrounding me on every side,
They pounce on me and press
Like a greedy lion lurching
From its dark recess,

Watching me to fathom how
They'll cast me to the ground –
Confront them, Lord, and rescue me:
In you my hope is found!
Send your sword to save me
And deliver me from death;
Take me from their evil grasp
And from their foul breath!

Their bellies fat with treasures,
For you keep them well-supplied,
Their children in abundance
Gaining all they've laid aside.
I'll inherit none of this,
Yet better is my prize:
When I wake, I'll be content
To look upon your eyes.

18

Lord, my strength, it's you I love:
The crag on which I rest,
The fortress that surrounds me
And delivers me when pressed,
The rock that is my refuge,
And the shield in which I hide,
The horn that sends salvation,
And the house where I abide.

I cried out in my anguish, Lord,
Assaulted by my foes;
The nets of death entangled me,
The roaring torrent rose;
I was tightly fastened
To the dragnets of the Pit,
And pulled in – by the snares
Of deadly evil caught and bit.

In distress I called to you,
I wept in my great woe;
My cry came up to your high place –
You saved me from my foe.
Hearing in your Temple vast
My little plea for help,
You roared out in your anger,
Swift to save this meagre whelp.

The Earth itself was reeling:
Mighty mountains, trembling, shook;
With fire and smoke you set ablaze
The kindled ground to cook –
Fire from your nostrils blazed,
You split the sky in two,
And came down to the Earth –
On soaring cherubim you flew,

Riding on the wind you came,
Thick darkness at your feet,
And as a cloak about you was
The darkness made complete.
Waters black from clouds like coals
Came raining from the sky,
With hailstones like burning rocks
That fell as you passed by,

For your fearsome presence
Was too bright for us to see,
And your voice as thunder burst
To make the wicked flee.
You sent out swift arrows
To disperse them like the dust,
You hurled spears of lightning down
Which through their hearts did thrust;

The very springs that feed the oceans
In the depths exposed,
The very Earth's foundations
Were uncovered when you rose

And in your fierce displeasure spoke
To roast them with rebuke;
As for me, you took me up
And saved me by no fluke –

You reached down from the heavens,
Drew me safe from roaring seas,
And saved me from my fierce foes,
My mighty enemies.
They pounced on me to take me
In the day of my distress,
But the Lord upheld me
From all those who would oppress.

He brought me into freedom,
As my life was His delight;
With good things He rewards those
Who are righteous in His sight.
He noticed that my hands were clean,
That I had kept His ways,
And had not wandered wickedly
To spurn Him, all my days:

I held my eye upon His law,
All His commandments kept;
I served the Lord wholeheartedly,
My goodness never slept.
Therefore was His recompense most kind,
Since I was clean –
By the faithful and the true
God's faith and truth is seen.

To the pure our God is pure,
The lowly ones He saves,
But to the crooked He will send
Adversity in waves:
He will bring the haughty down,
The high looks of the proud;
As for me, His candle's light
Will pierce my dark night's shroud.

I shall have no fear of mine enemy,
But run
Straight into the fiercest host,
Against both sword and gun,
And leap atop the highest fence,
For God is at my side:
God, His way is perfect,
His true word by fire tried.

He will be a shield
Guarding all who trust His word –
Who is God, the rock on which we stand,
Except the Lord?
It is God who gives me strength,
Who sets my way aright;
It is God who lets me walk
With ease the greatest height,
Who gives me feet like mountain goats',
Who trains my hands for war,
Who makes mine arms to bend
A bow of bronze with arrows sure.

The shield of salvation
Keeps me safe from all assault;
Your right hand and grace, O God,
Keep me from every fault.
You make me stride with ease the land
On feet that do not trip;
I pursue my foes
That from my grasp they shall not slip.

I shall not turn again
Till I destroy them, gone complete:
I smite them so they shall not rise,
They fall beneath my feet.
You give me strength for battle,
It is you who strikes them down,
And those that hated me turn tail
And run from your renown.

When they cry there is no help –
Perhaps they cry to you,
But you will not answer those
Who your ways never knew.
I shall cast them down as dung,
Shall grind them into sand;
You shall set me up as head,
Above them all to stand,

Delivered from their pointless strife:
The people shall obey,
Though I have not known them,
They shall all do as I say,
Humbled there before me –
In their strivings they lose heart,
And from their strongholds trembling
Fall to hear what I impart.

Blessed be my rock, my God
Who lives for evermore;
Praisèd be my God whose great
Salvation now is sure –
God it is who vindicated me,
Who will subdue
All the many peoples of the Earth:
They hark to you,

You who have delivered me,
Set high above my foes;
You who drove their violence from me,
Turnèd back their blows;
You whom I shall thank, O God,
And sing with endless praise;
You who rescued me,
And me above the lowly raise;
You who gave great victory
To help your king indeed:
You pour out faithful love upon
King David and his seed!

19

The heavens recount the glory of God!
Mere space sings out His praise;
Knowledge is unfolded,
Shared out through all nights and days,

Though they have no words nor tongue,
Nor speak with any voice,
Still across the whole wide world
We hear them, and rejoice

Because their sound reverberates,
In every land begun
Where goes the travelling tabernacle,
Dwelling of the Sun.

She comes forth in the morning
Like the bridegroom from his room,
Or like the racing champion
Who takes delight to zoom

From one end of the heavens
To the very end again:
So the Sun the sky patrols
And pours her golden rain.

The Lord's law is a perfect law,
The soul it can revive;
His testimony certain,
Making wisdom come alive;

The statutes of the Lord are good
And right, rejoicing hearts,
And light fills up their lives
Through all that His command imparts.

The fear of God is clean and holy,
Endless it endures;
True and righteous are the judgements
That the Lord assures.

More are they to be desired
Than all the finest gold,
Sweeter still than any sweetness
Dripping honey holds.

By them is your servant taught,
Keeping good accord,
And in those righteous judgements
There is very great reward.

Who can say how often one offends,
And breaks your law?
Wash from me the secret faults
That blemish me for sure.

Make me not presumptuous,
And cleanse me from my sins,
Lest evil's domination
Of this feeble soul begins!

Then shall I be not defiled
By any filthy deed;
Then, accused of great offence,
I innocent may plead.

Let my words, my meditations deep,
Be good and right,
Be found to be acceptable
And precious in your sight.

20

May the Lord be listening
When your life hangs by a thread,
May His help come swiftly
From His sanctuary's gates.
May His shield defend you
In the troubled paths you tread:
May the God who Jacob led
Remember him that waits,

Who sent the sweetest offerings
In scented smoke on high,
Who sacrificed the best
Of all the bounty you received –
May the Lord remember you,
Send blessings from the sky,
And grant you all your heart's desire,
All that your mind conceived.

May we who see rejoice
In your salvation from the Lord,
And triumph that our God's great name
Not vainly is invoked –
Now I know that God gives
His anointed their reward;
From the highest heaven He has answered,
And revoked

The pompous power of those
Who in their chariots put trust,
While on the only God in heaven
We in faith do call –
They are smashed and broken,
All their iron turned to rust,
But God will save us as our King:
With Him, we shall not fall.

21

O Lord, the King's rejoicing
In your saving strength is great:
You have not denied him,
Or made his perfection wait,
But gave him all his heart's desire –
Blessings did you hold,
Coming down to set
Upon his head a crown of gold.

He asked of you his life, you gave it –
And great length of days;
Majesty and glory
Have you laid on him always.
Because of your salvation, Lord,
Much honour now he holds;
Felicity for ever
Through your gracious gift unfolds.

By your very presence
You will fill his heart with joy;
He who trusts in God alone
No foe will dare destroy.
All of those who hate you, Lord,
Your hand will find and mark,
Burned up by a great inferno
Lighted by your spark:

As a fiery oven
You will swallow them with wrath,
And fire will consume all those
Who block your holy path.
All their fruit is rotten;
You will root it out for good,
And burn away their wicked seed
Like so much kindled wood.

They intended evil,
They cooked up such wicked schemes,
But they cannot carry out
Their sordid plots it seems:
You have overpowered them,
They fled before your face;
when you aim your bow at them
They shrivel in disgrace.

We exalt you, mighty God –
Beyond each hill and tower,
Melody and song ascend
To tell of your great power!

22

O God, my God, you are my God:
    Why do you forsake me?
    Why do you not answer
    In my hour of distress?

They press me round, they stab my side,
    They crush my bones and break me;
    With parchèd mouth in agony
    I drink the dust of death.

Day by day I cry in vain, at night I find no rest;
    With wicked words they pour out scorn
        and slander in the street.
    It was you who nurtured me,
        from on my mother's breast –
'Where is now the Lord he loved?'
    with lying lips they bleat.

Oh God! They stand and stare at me,
    and mock my withered frame:
Naked now, they nail me up and take my clothes by lot.
Why do you not answer, when I call upon your name?
    You've set me 'midst a pack of hounds
        And I am clean forgot.

The raging lions close to kill –
and you answer me!
Oh God, my God, I shout your praise:
it echoes round the Earth!
Every nation, every kingdom
Now will bend the knee,
For countless generations yet,
To see their blessed birth!

Your ears you have not hardened
to the crying of the poor;
The wicked will not praise you
as their bones go back to dust;
Those who sing your name
will sing your praise for evermore,
And glorify the gracious God
Whose wondrous deeds we trust!

23

The Lord, as my most loving shepherd
Leads me in His flock;
I can lack for nothing when
I trust in God my rock.

He lets me lie in pastures green,
The garden of delight,
And graze beside still waters
Fresh and glistening in my sight.

My soul He will refresh, refined
With waters cool and pure;
On His paths He guides me,
And through danger brings me sure.

Though I walk through death's dark valley,
Where fell shadows lie,
I will fear no evil one,
Nor tremble that I die.

For you, my God, are with me –
I hold fast your rod and staff;
These will be my comfort
On the straight and narrow path.

Deep precipices fall away –
On either side they gape,
But you, O God, will keep me:
You have fashioned my escape.

You spread a table rich and fair
That we, your flock, may feast;
The enemies who troubled me look on,
Their jibing ceased.

You anoint my head with oil,
You my cup will fill;
Your sweet love and mercy
Will I drink deep at your will.

Goodness, it will follow me
And bless my life's long days
And I will dwell for ever
Where your blissful spirit stays.

24

All the Earth belongs to God,
And all that fills it too;
All those who inhabit its
Wide compass does He keep.
He founded land upon the shores
Of His vast ocean blue
And set it on its firm foundations –
Rivers of the deep.

Who now shall ascend His hill,
May rise up in His place?
Those whose hearts were wholly love,
Whose hands were clean of sin,
Who never swore a lying oath,
Will see His blessed face –
Who to lift their souls to idols
Never did begin.

Theirs shall be a just reward;
From God they will receive,
Who sought to see their Lord's salvation
And His blessing win:
This is that great company,
Brought up from those who grieve,
To see the gates uplifted
And the King of Might come in.

Who is this King of Glory?
'Tis the Lord who ends all wars,
The Lord most strong and mighty
Who this battle soon will win!
Lift your heads, O gates;
Crash down, you everlasting doors!
Make way and open
For the King of Glory shall come in!

25

To you, O Lord, I lift my soul:
My God, in you I trust.
O let me not be shamed
Before the enemy's cruel thrust!

Let none who look to you
Be put to shame before their foes,
But the cruel and treacherous –
Their graceless deeds expose!

Make me know your paths, O Lord,
And teach me all your ways:
Lead me into truth and show me
How to live my days.

You are my salvation,
All day long my only hope:
Call to mind compassion;
For your loving help I grope –

They are everlasting mercies,
Steadfast and secure;
Remember not my youthful sins
And faults for evermore.

Think on me in goodness:
God so gracious, just and true,
You will teach to sinners
All the things they ought to do.

You will show the humble
And the lonely what is right;
All your ways are merciful
To those who seek your light,

Who keep your laws, your covenant,
Your testimony wise –
Have mercy on my sin,
For it is great before mine eyes!

Those who fear the Lord
He tells the way that they should choose;
Their souls are set at ease
As on His covenant they muse.

His hidden purpose is revealed
To those who trust the Lord;
Their offspring shall inherit
All the land as their reward.

Mine eyes are ever looking to my God:
I sink in sin,
But He will swoop and pluck me
From the net I'm tangled in.

O God, my spirit sinks,
And I am left here all alone:
Turn now in your grace to save me,
Hear my desperate groan!

The sorrows of my heart increase,
I break beneath their weight;
I am brought down very low
To dark despair's fell gate.

Look on mine adversity,
My misery and pain;
Cleanse me of my sin –
Forgive, and bring me up again.

See, the strutting enemies are many,
All about,
With violence they strike at me,
With hatred do they shout.

Keep me and deliver me,
I put my trust in you –
Preserve me in integrity,
Let righteousness hold true.

All our hope in you is founded,
Trusting you to save –
Deliver Israel from the storm
And troubles of the grave.

26

I have trusted you, O Lord:
Give judgement now for me;
I have not turned nor stumbled,
Walking with integrity.
Examine all my heart and soul –
O put me to the test;
Try my mettle in the fire,
You'll find it of the best.

I look with eyes of love for you,
And to your truth I hold;
I have not kept vain company
With those whose hearts are cold,
Nor joined with the deceivers
To consort in their cruel deeds:
I will not sit and revel
With that patch of wicked weeds!

I wash my hands of wickedness,
I come before you clean
To pay you thanks and sing of all
Your gracious works I've seen,
To serve before your altar
And my life's oblations give:
Lord I love the holy habitation
Where you live!

Do not root me out
With all the bloodthirsty and base;
Do not sweep me up
With all the sinners in disgrace!
Their hands work schemes of evil,
Open only for a bribe
And stained by blood of innocents
They've broken to imbibe.

God, my steps are not with them:
By righteous paths I tread –
Be merciful, redeem me
For the little blood I've shed.
My foot will find a solid rock
From which I shall not fall,
And in the congregation I will bless you,
Standing tall.

27

The Lord, He is my lantern,
  My salvation and my light:
So that I shall have no fear,
  Not in the darkest night.

The Lord, He is my help,
The strength on which my life is staid:
  Who, then, could endanger me
  Or make me feel afraid?

The wicked came upon me,
  All mine enemies and foes:
They thought they could consume me
  With the power of their blows,

But in sin they stumbled
  And upon their folly fell:
For all my trust is in the Lord
  And He has kept me well.

Though encamped against me comes
  A vast and mighty host,
Though they seek to summon war,
  I quake not at their boast:

One thing have I asked of God,
  That He may end such strife,
And I may dwell within His house
  All through my days of life,

To behold His beauty
And to strive to do His will:
This alone is my desire,
And I seek it still.

In the day of trouble
He shall hide me from the fight,
In His secret shelter,
On a rock in some great height:

He shall lift my head
Above mine enemies all round;
I shall offer in His house
Such gladness as I've found.

I shall sing with music,
With sweet praises to the Lord –
Hear my voice and answer me,
Do not hold back your sword!

In my heart I know your word,
It tells me, 'seek my face' –
Your face, Lord, will I seek out;
O give me not disgrace!

Cast me not away
Nor turn your face from me, O God:
You have been my only help,
Take not your guiding rod!

My mother and my father
May forsake me in disgust,
But God will not forsake me:
On His steadfast love I trust.

Lord, lead me on a level path
And teach me all your ways:
Let me not fall victim
To the ambush evil lays.

False witnesses have risen up
Against me in the court –
Save me from their will,
For lies and violence they snort.

I believe that I shall see
The goodness of the Lord,
Even in the land of life:
This shall be my reward.

Trust the Lord and wait for Him,
Be strong and lose not heart;
Wait patiently for God, for He
Your comfort will impart.

28

O Lord, you are the rock
On which I stand: to you I cry;
Do not let my call
Of desperation pass you by.

If you do not hear me,
If you turn your ear away,
I shall fall into
The very deepest pit this day.

Hear my humble prayer,
Lest I join the souls of death,
When I lift my hands to you
And sputter longing breath.

O please, Lord, snatch me not away
With all the wicked men;
Nor list me with the evildoers
Marked down by your pen –

Those who utter buttered speech,
With malice in their hearts;
Reward them for the sordid outcome
Of their evil arts!

Pay to them their just deserts,
Who pay no heed to you,
Who care not for your wondrous works
And press your people too.

You will break their pillars down
And will not raise them up,
Who set themselves above the rest
And pour a poisoned cup.

Blessed be the Lord my God,
Who heard my meagre voice,
Who helped me in my trouble
Since His trust has been my choice;

The Lord is both my members' strength
And my poor body's shield –
A refuge for His people,
Who salvation's sword doeth wield.

For this cause my heartbeat skips,
My mouth is full of praise:
With joy my soul is dancing,
For He speaks of better days.

God, now save your people –
Bless the heritage you gave,
And be their constant shepherd
Even yet beyond the grave.

29

Ascribe to God, celestial powers,
Glory, might and strength!
Ascribe to God, the Lord alone,
Throughout creation's length,
The honour that we owe to Him,
His name our duty's pull:
Worship Him whose holiness
In wholly beautiful!

God is on the waters:
Hear His mighty voice ring out;
The God of Glory thunders
From the booming water-spout;
Mighty is its operation,
Glorious is its sound:
Trees will break and tremble
Where the Lord's great voice is found.

Lebanon and Sirion
Skip like a wild ox,
His lightning flashes split the sky,
The wilderness He rocks!
He shakes the ground to splinters
As He strips the forests bare;
Even oak trees writhe and sway
Because God's voice is there.

In His Temple all cry 'Glory!'
Where He sits on high;
Enthroned as King for ever
Over water flood and sky.
He gives strength to His people,
Making all their strivings cease,
And for the straits of torment
Showers blessings of His peace.

30

My God, I will exalt you:
You have raised me up on High,
Nor left me 'neath mine enemies'
Triumphant feet to lie.

O God, when I cried out to you,
You heard and healed my pain;
You took me out of death's dark vale
And brought me up again.

You lifted me to life
Amidst those destined for the Pit,
And with your servants I will sing
And give you thanks for it!

Your wrath is but a moment,
For the twinkling of an eye;
Your favour lasts a lifetime
And you hear the humble cry:

The heavy weight of sadness
May endure for a night,
But joy returns to fill my heart
When breaks the morning light!

In my vain prosperity, I said
'I shall not fall,
For God in His great goodness
Keeps me safe from perils all.'

Then you hid your favour –
I was cast into dismay,
When to you I cried
And in my sorry state did say,

'What, Lord, would it profit you,
To put me in the Pit?
Will the dust declare your praise
When I by death am bit?

'Hear, O Lord, and help me:
Pour your mercy on my soul,
Boil not my blood away
But dowse the burning coal!'

You turned my mournful darkness
Into dancing all the day;
With gladness you have girded me,
My sackcloth cast away,

And so my heart, not ceasing,
Will its songs of praises send,
And I will thank my Lord and God,
World without an end!

31

Let them not ashame me, Lord:
My refuge is in you;
I trusted in your righteousness
To safely bring me through.
Incline thine ear and hear me:
Deliver me in haste,
Be my firm foundation
And my fortress from disgrace!

Yes, you are my fast escape,
My stronghold and my rock;
Be my guide, and lead me,
Open up to me the lock
By which they tried to trap me,
With a net beneath my feet:
For in you alone, O God,
My strength is made complete.

Into your embracing hands
My spirit I commend,
For you have redeemed me, Lord,
My true and only friend.
Those who cling to idols
That are worthless, I renounce:
I weigh out my trust
And give to God my every ounce!

In your loving mercy, I rejoice:
My heart is glad;
You saw me in affliction,
Knew my soul's distress was bad,
And did not let mine enemy
Strike with his wicked hand –
You drew me from his talons,
In an open place I stand.

Have mercy on me, Lord,
For now my trouble presses sore:
My body heaves with sorrow
And mine eyes with tears are raw;
My life is wasted with my grief,
My years used up with sighs;
And now my strength is failing
And my frame disjointed lies.

To every near neighbour
I am made a sore reproach,
And my old acquaintances,
They shrink at my approach.
When they see me in the street
They turn the other way;
As if I were an enemy,
For my decease they pray.

I am now forgotten
As the dead, beyond recall,
Like a broken vessel
On the granite floor I fall,

And I hear their whispers:
Words of fear on every side,
As they speak against me,
Plot to take me in their pride,
And crush my life from in me –
So they scheme, this wicked crowd,
But I have trusted you, O God,
To wrap me in your shroud.

All my time is at your touch,
And you can make me whole:
Take me from my persecutors,
Save my worried soul!
Make your face to shine
Upon your servant with a smile;
For your loving mercy's sake
My strait do not revile!

Do not let me be undone:
I called upon your name;
Let instead the wicked
Go to silence in their shame.
Let their lips be stopped
Who hold the righteous in contempt,
In arrogance and haughtiness,
With ugly words unkempt.

Your goodness, Lord, is laid up
For your servants in great store;
You made it plain that you prepared
Abundant grace and more
For those that put their trust in you –
You shelter them from harm,
You keep them safe in refuge
From all slander and alarm.

Blessed be the Lord –
I like a city was besieged,
But in His steadfast love
All of my troubles are relieved.
In my panicked plight I thought
You'd lost me from your sight,
But you heard my prayerful plea
And took me up by night.

Love the Lord, His servants,
For the faithful He protects;
He repays the proud
For all their cruelty and neglect.
Be strong and let your heart take courage –
Great is your reward,
All who wait in hope,
Who put their trust upon the Lord.

32

How happy is the heart of one
Whose sins are swept away,
Whose trespass is forgiven,
Who have no great price to pay,
For God imputes no guilt on them,
Washed clean are they of guile:
God forgives their wretchedness,
And makes sad faces smile.

When I held my tongue,
I dared not whisper of my wrong:
Then my bones were wasted
In my anguish, all day long;
Your heavy hand opprest me
Like a weight by day and night;
I withered as in summer's heat
Beneath your searching light.

Then, I uttered painful words,
I spoke out of my sin;
I hid no more my feelings,
To repentance I gave in.
I said, 'I shall confess it all:
I've no more strength to lie,'
So I spilled my heart to you,
And piled my failings high.

You took one look upon me, Lord,
And I expected wrath;
But pity was your answer,
As you blew away the chaff.
Lord, I learnt to love you
And in trouble seek you out,
A happy place to hide in
When the wicked stalk about.

Let the faithful turn to you in prayer,
Come the storm;
The flood, it shall not reach them,
And their fate be not forlorn.
You surround me with your songs,
You teach me where to go;
You guide me with your watchful eye
That wisdom I may know.

You made me not as horse and mule
Who wander from the way,
Who must be held with bit and bridle
Lest they go astray.
You told me, only trust the Lord
And mercy will be mine:
The wicked sink amidst their strife,
The righteous will be fine.

Be glad, you righteous, and rejoice
In God: shout out for joy,
For any who are true of heart
The Lord will not destroy.

33

Rejoice in God, you righteous ones:
    To pour out praise is good!
Praise the Lord with harp and lyre,
    Praise with brass and wood!

Play to Him with all your skill,
    And sing His songs anew,
For the works of God are sure,
    The words of God are true.

He delights in righteousness,
    With justice is His joy;
He filled the Earth so full with love,
    And kindness did employ:

By His breath alone
    The whole of Heaven's host was made;
The ocean's breadth and depth
    Within His treasury is laid.

He gathers them as in a cup,
    The waters of the sea:
He only has to speak by His command,
    And it will be.

All the Earth should stand in awe,
    Its peoples bow in fear,
For the Lord who brings the nations' plans
    To naught is near:

He cancels all their counsels,
He frustrates their vain designs,
But happy are the peoples
On whom His instruction shines.

The plans imparted by the Lord,
His counsels, never fail –
Though many generations pass,
His help does not grow stale.

Happy are the peoples
He has chosen for His own,
As He looks upon the Earth
And sees His children roam,

And beholds the hearts of men
And sees their every work:
From His gaze upon His throne,
No hidden secrets lurk.

A king cannot be saved by might
Nor multitude of host;
Let no Earthly warrior
In strength or cunning boast.

You cannot hope a horse will save you –
For its strength and speed,
Deliverance from God
Cannot be won by any steed.

God's eye rests on those who fear Him:
Watching from above,
He rescues all who hope in Him
And in His steadfast love.

He feeds them in the famine,
He holds back their soul from death;
Our heart in Him rejoices,
By whose grace we draw each breath.

Our soul waits longingly for Him,
Who is our help and shield:
Let your love and kindness, Lord,
Before us be revealed!

34

Let my mouth be filled with praise,
My loosened tongue confess,
The gracious glory of my God
Whom I am glad to bless.

O, magnify the Lord with me:
Exalt His mighty name;
But look upon His light
And let your face shine out the same!

In sore distress I sought Him,
And from fear He set me free;
He scattered all the troubles
And assailants pressing me.

Before His angels, vaunted foes
Will run away and hide;
Evil slays the wicked,
While the righteous long abide.

Would you wish for rest and peace,
Delight in happy days?
Listen to the Lord your God
And walk in all His ways.

His children never hunger,
For He gives them all that's good:
The proud who seek things for themselves
Have never understood

That God rewards the righteous –
He will hear them when they call;
The humble are contented,
While the mighty thirst and fall.

Turn from evil, practise good,
And keep your tongue from lies:
Though many be your troubles,
God will dry your teary eyes.

Though your heart be broken,
And your spirit sorely pressed,
Still the Lord is near you,
And with Him will be your rest.

He won't let a single bone
Of your blest body break,
Perfect will He raise the righteous:
Ransomed, they awake.

Though many be your adversaries,
God will slay them all –
They will be forgotten,
But the righteous never fall.

35

Contend with those who would contend
And fight with those who fight:
Come, Lord, to my rescue
With your sword and shield of might.

Draw your spear and bar the way
To those who hunt me down,
Be my soul's salvation
And protect me lest I drown!

Let those who seek my life
Be made ashamed of what they've done,
Those who plot to ruin me
Into destruction run!

May God's angel thrust them down
To fall back in disgrace,
Let them fly as chaff
Upon the wind before your face.

Let them flee in fear down alleys
Slippery and black,
While God's angel in pursuit
Approaches to attack.

They have spread a net for me,
To catch without a cause;
They have dug a pit for me
To snare me in their gauze;

Let ruin fall upon their heads –
Into the net they laid
Let them fall to their destruction,
Since on me they preyed.

Then my soul will sing for joy,
Salvation will be mine;
My very bones will sing to God,
'Whose glory is as thine?

'You save the weak and feeble poor
From those who are too strong,
Who seek to spoil the needy
And care not that they do wrong.'

False witnesses arose against me,
Blackening my name
With charge of things that I knew not
They'd cover me with shame!

They sought to desolate my soul,
Gave evil for my good;
While I when they were sick had wept
And in rough sackcloth stood.

I with humble fasting
For their healing made my prayer;
I mourned as for my mother
When no better did they fare;

I grieved as for my friend or brother,
    Brought down very low –
Yet when I tripped they pushed me down
    And bitter was their blow.

They gathered round as wicked vultures,
    Happy at my plight;
    They tore at me as if
They did not know me, in delight;

    When I fell they laughed at me
    And gnashed their greedy teeth,
        Acting as my enemies
    They revelled in my grief.

    Lord, how long will you look on
        And let the lions roar?
    Rescue me from ravaging –
        Behold, my plight is poor!

        In the congregation
    I will always give you thanks;
        I will sing your praises
    From amidst the mighty ranks.

        Do not let such villains
        In their treachery rejoice:
    Those who hate me with no cause
        Assault me with their voice

Or mock me with their glances,
For of peace they never speak,
But summon up such wicked schemes
Against the poor and meek.

They opened wide their mouths and said,
'We saw it with our eyes!'
But you look down and know, O God,
That all their words were lies.

Please, do not keep silent
When destruction fills my ears;
Do not depart and leave me, Lord,
To cry my bitter tears.

Awake and rise to plead my cause,
And come to my defence;
Give me justice
With your righteous words of recompense!

Do not let them triumph, saying,
'We shall swallow him!
Let us have our heart's desire!'
As they do me in.

Let all those who glee to see
My trouble come to shame:
Put them to confusion,
All who falsely lay the blame,

Who boast themselves against me –
May dishonour be their end;
Let them know no gladness,
Let them fall without a friend.

Those who love me say,
'How great is God: for He delights
To save His servants' health and life
And put all wrongs to rights!'

My tongue shall talk of all your deeds,
Your righteousness so sure,
And all day long my praise shall be
To God forever more.

36

When the wicked hear the whisper
of temptation in their heart,
Do they think that God is blind,
Or will not see their sin?
Do they think to fool Him
By their frail human art,
And by their vain, deceitful mouths
Their filthy souls to win?

Oh, you who plot oppression,
Nor hold back from evil deeds,
Be gone from me, who'd have me stumble
On the foot of pride!
God it is, not man,
Who every living creature feeds;
In His warm embrace,
Beneath His sheltering wings, I'll hide.

God, whose love is infinite,
Above the highest cloud,
Beyond the furthest reaches
Of the dark's sky's endless deep –
He will wrap all mortal flesh
Within His loving shroud;
In His house for ever
Will we be content to sleep.

Light of lights,
The source from whom the well of life is sprung,
Who in His loving mercy
Lets the faithful drink their fill,
Let me not be led astray
Nor heed the lying tongue
Of the proud, who helpless fall
Before your mighty will!

37

The wicked try to threaten you
Or tempt you from the way;
They seem at first to know success,
But for their deeds they'll pay.
Their glory's like the meadow flowers
That brightly bloom in June,
But fade beneath the summer sun
And vanish all too soon.

Like smoke ascending to the sky,
Dissolved without a trace,
So will all the wicked be among the human race.
They plot against the righteous,
As they gnash their fierce teeth;
God laughs at their petty threats –
He knows their time is brief.

They glower down upon the poor
To strike with sword and bow,
But even as they thrust,
He turns on them their cruel blow.
God will snap their swords to splinters,
All their wealth will rust;
Far greater riches have the poor
When in the Lord they trust.

Those who ravished through their greed,
Giving nothing back,
Will be left with nothing,
Whilst the righteous never lack:
All day long the righteous give
Of what they have received;
Their children never hunger,
And their souls are never grieved.

Once I was a young man,
Now my body waxes old;
But I have never seen the good
To beggary be sold.

When God directs your footsteps,
Sheer delight will gird your path,
Because the Lord loves righteousness
But evil stirs His wrath.
Your mouth will brim with wisdom,
And your heart will hold His law;
With the Lord to hold you up
Your footing shall be sure.

He will give you goodly lands,
The wicked He'll uproot,
Who stand now strong and flourishing
But will not bear their fruit
Before they're gone and vanished –
they are nowhere to be found:
Their own cruel and selfish deeds
Upon their heads rebound.

Follow not in crooked ways,
For at their end is death;
Trust the Lord in innocence
And He will give you breath
And snatch you from the grasping hands
Of those who spy and plot,
Safe within His stronghold
While disaster strikes the lot.

Never follow wickedness,
Which wins its own reward:
If you long for peace and length of days,
Embrace the Lord.

38

Lord, do not rebuke me –
Do not cast me to the dust,
Nor chasten me so harshly
In displeasure and disgust.
The arrows of your anger sharp
Lord, I cannot abide,
And from your hand that presses hard
I have no place to hide.

My flesh is rotten and diseased,
My bones no peace may win,
Because you are indignant
At the tally of my sin.
My faults have overtaken me,
So deep above my head;
Their weight is such a heavy burden,
Bitterness and dread;

The wounds I have inflicted
On my own flesh, as a fool,
Start to stink and fester
Like a stagnant, toxic pool.
I bow beneath this weight of sins,
They bring me very low:
All day long in mourning
And in misery I go.

My joints erupt in searing pain,
My flesh has now no health;
Completely crushed and smashed to pieces
Is my meagre self.
I roar aloud in agony,
My heart can find no rest;
O Lord, you hear my sighs incessant
And my pounding chest!

You know my inmost thoughts
And the desire of my mind:
Help me, for my strength has failed;
Mine eyes are rendered blind.
My friends and my companions
And my neighbours stand far off,
Apart from mine affliction,
While my foes look on and scoff.

They seek my life, they lay down snares,
They slander with their tongue;
Those who seek to harm me
Whisper evil all day long.
I, like one who cannot hear,
Am deaf to what they say;
Like one who cannot speak
I do not answer their affray.

Like one made deaf and mute, my mouth
Will utter no retort:
For in you is my trust, O God,
And your help have I sought.

Let them not in triumph stand
Above me and exult,
Who long to see my footing slip
And yearn to find my fault!
I have nearly fallen, Lord:
I scramble at the verge;
My pain is ever present
As a deep and constant dirge;

I will confess iniquity,
Be sorry for my sin,
But those who hate me wrongfully
Surround and hem me in!
Many is their number,
And so mighty is their threat:
Those who without any cause
As foes themselves have set,

Who spurn the good I showed them,
Giving evil in its place:
Because I sought for righteousness
They hold me in disgrace!
Lord, do not forsake me –
Be not far from me, O God –
Make haste to help and save me,
O my refuge and my rod!

39

I said, 'I shall tread carefully,
Keep watch over my ways –
With the wicked listening
One must take care what one says.
I'll guard my mouth as with a muzzle,
Making no offence,
And tie my tongue –
As though they did no wrong I'll make pretence.'

So I kept my silence
And said nothing, but in vain:
Hot anger burned within my heart,
I could not bear the pain.
Musing on their evil deeds,
So great was my distress
I had no choice but to speak out
And my complaint express.

'Lord, I wish to live no longer:
Let me know mine end;
Let me know my life's extent,
My days' sad number end.
You have made my span so short,
My life to you is naught:
Even those with righteous hearts
By death so soon are caught.

'As shadows to the rising Sun
We walk about – a breath;
In vain our trials and torment
In this life whose end is death.
We toil to heap up riches
That we live not to enjoy –
Deliver me from mockery,
And my proud sins destroy!

'Now what is my hope?
My only hope, O Lord, is you.'
So I fell to silence,
My lips again like glue.
Yet take away this plague from me –
By your blows I'm consumed;
With rebuke you punish me
For sin – am I yet doomed?

Like a moth you eat my beauty,
Youth gone like a sigh:
Hear my prayer and answer, Lord,
Be not deaf to my cry!
Do not hold your peace
And watch my bitter tears pour:
Ere I go away to nothing,
And become no more,

Turn your angry gaze from me
And make me glad again,
For I am but a stranger
In this wicked world of men.

40

Through the night's long watches
I was waiting for the Lord:
In patient faith I waited,
And He gave me my reward.
He inclined His ear to me –
My cry came to His ears,
And He has banished all my nightmares,
All my greatest fears.

In the mire I could not move;
I could not climb the clay,
But He did lift me on a rock
Far from the fiery fray;
Far above the frightful pit
He made my footing sure,
And now a new song do I sing
Of praise for evermore.

Those who see me fear Him –
In the Lord they put their trust,
And blessed is the one who follows Him,
Most true and just.
The proud put faith in vain pursuits
And find they are but lies;
Great, though, are the wonders
God has wrought before our eyes!

There is none compared with Him –
I have no words to tell
Of all His great designs for us,
So vast His love's deep well!
Sacrifice and offerings
He has not asked of me,
To scrub away my sin that I
May clean before Him be,

But He has whispered in mine ears
Wisdom of the Truth:
He knows I will not hold my tongue
Nor ever stand aloof,
But shout of His salvation,
Love and faithfulness, and sing
Before the congregation,
Not concealing any thing.

In your book, my name is writ,
That I should do your will;
And it is my heart's delight,
O God, to serve you still.
Your law lies deep within me;
Deliver me and help,
And have compassion on your servant –
On this meagre whelp.

Let your love and faithfulness
Preserve me on the way;
Deliver me, who sang your praise,
In the distressful day!

Troubles overwhelm me;
In my own sin do I sink;
They press so hard upon my head
I cannot stand, nor think;
For they are more in number
Than the hairs upon my scalp:
In my tears, my heart is drowned –
I call to you for help!

Let them be ashamèd
Who have sought to take my life;
Let them be upbraided
Who bring on me hurt and strife;
May they who heap up insults
Like hot coals upon the fire
Feel the shame and desolation
Of your fearsome ire!

But we who seek to serve you, Lord,
Let us rejoice – be glad,
And sing your gracious praise
For the salvation we have had.
I may be poor and needy,
But the Lord will be my stay:
He will feed and shelter me.
O God, do not delay!

You alone, my helper,
Are the one who shows me care:
Be my swift deliverer,
And save me from despair!

41

The Lord will bless the one
Who lends the poor and needy aid:
In their time of trouble
He will save them in their turn –
The Lord protects and prospers them,
Though adverse foes invade:
He will not hand them over
To the will of those they spurn.

Even on the sickbed He sustains them,
Gives them health,
Restores them to utility,
Removes the ills they bear.
And so I said 'be merciful
To my own sinful self,'
Acknowledging my hurt to Him
And pleading for repair.

Mine enemies speak evil things:
They ponder my demise,
They say they hope to see me dead,
My name be blotted out;
They utter empty words to me,
Who in their heart despise,
And in the broad streets spread
Their wicked rumours all about.

They whisper evil words together,
Plotting for my death;
They say a deadly thing
Has taken hold of my poor heart,
That whence I lie I shall not rise,
But take my final breath –
Even he, my oldest friend,
Has set himself apart.

He ate my bread and shared my secrets,
Even from my youth,
Who lifts up now his heel
That he might strike me in the face.
But you, O Lord, be merciful –
You know I speak the truth;
Raise me up that I may live
To recompense this race.

I know that you will favour me,
Because they triumph not,
Because in mine integrity
Me from the brink you bring –
You will set me in your presence,
While the wicked rot:
O blessed be the God of Israel,
Everlasting King!

42

Just as the thirsty deer longs after water,
So does my soul seek for you, O my God.
I cry, like a mother who mourns for her daughter;
I sob out my soul to see where I once trod

When with you beside me I led the procession,
The multitude cheering me up to your house.
Now they have stripped me of every possession;
Now they reject me, expunged like a louse.

O God, I drink tears, and choke on my crying –
My soul is so heavy, it plummets like lead.
O God, why forget me? Why leave me here dying?
'Where is this God that you trust in?' they said.

They beat on my bones as they crush me and mock me,
'Where is your God to protect you?' they say.
Lord, in the night-time your sweet song will rock me,
Your kindness will comfort me all through the day.

God, your great waves have washed over me throughly,
The deep places echo your thundering voice.
God, they oppress me; I trust in you truly:
To give you my thanks is my only free choice.

Thanks, though my heart it can help not but plummet,
Thanks, though my soul in great tumult abides:
High is the rock of your great strength's bright summit,
And safe is the soul that in your mercy hides.

43

Deliver me, O God! Deceit and wickedness oppress me –
O leave me not alone within a land that loves you not.
This people does not know you;
With your righteous judgement bless me,
For you alone will be my refuge
When their hand strikes hot.

Send out for me a ray of light to lead me in your way;
Bring me to your holy hill and help me up its height
That I may step into your house and at your altar pray,
And sing with joy and gladness
As I thank you for that sight!

Yet you cast me off, and so my soul will tremble still,
Weighed down while I bear
The heavy weight of all my woes.
O, put your trust in God, my soul: wait upon His will,
For surely He will lift you up
And save you from your foes.

44

We hear them tell of ancient days,
Of all you did of old –
Of how you drove out nations
That your name might take a hold

By planting in this people
To proclaim your majesty:
You broke the power of hostile foes
And set our fathers free.

Their own strength could not save them,
Nor the weapons of the land,
But your bright light, it guided them;
You led them by the hand.

Your mighty arm, it scattered
All adversaries adrift,
You trod our foes beneath our feet
And us with grace did lift.

We put no faith in sword nor bow,
But trusted in your name;
You saved us from our enemies
And put them all to shame.

You are my King, you are my God,
To Jacob ever true:
All day long we sang your praise
And gloried, God, in you.

But now you have rejected us;
In shame we shrink away,
Our armies swept aside like ants,
Despoilèd every day.

We are like sheep for slaughter,
By our enemies enslaved,
And carried off to other nations
Wicked and depraved.

O God, how they deride us,
How they taunt us while we fail!
You sold us for a pittance,
Made no profit on the sale;

You made the name of Israel
Be a byword for disgrace;
They wag their heads and pour out scorn:
In shame I hide my face.

Daily my confusion mounts,
I stagger at the sight
Of all you brought upon us,
Though our hearts were ever right:

We did not forget you,
Nor dissemble from your way;
We never played the harlot,
Nor to falsehood went astray.

Did we bow to idols
And forget your glorious name?
Did we stretch our hands towards
Strange gods of evil fame?

Did we think you wouldn't search
The secrets of the heart?
You know we never left you,
It is you who made us part.

For your sake we are slaughtered daily
In the jackals' lair,
We cannot see the light of day,
For death's dark pall we bear.

Our soul is buried in the dust,
Our belly to the ground.
We wail and sob with grief;
You shut your ears to the sound!

Why are you asleep, O Lord?
Rise up now and awake:
O God, do not reject us: help us,
For your mercy's sake.

45

O mighty King, my soul's astir;
My tongue is tingling too:
Brims my heart with gladness
To be singing songs for you!
Gracious praises pour like ointment
From my ready pen,
For you are blest by God
To be the fairest of all men.

Set your sword upon you,
Gird your glory as your crown;
Ride on for righteousness and truth,
Most worthy of renown!
You prosper in humility,
Your throne is God's on high;
Righteousness your lasting love,
Iniquity thrust by,

Your right hand just and terrible,
Your arrows sharp and swift,
The peoples fall beneath
The righteous sceptre that you lift.
With the oil of gladness,
God anoints you over all;
With sweetly scented garments
In your majesty, stand tall!

Glad music pours from palaces,
From strings that sing for you,
For your Queen all decked in gold,
Your royal daughters too.
Listen to this music, foreign princess –
Bend your ear;
Forget your former family
And make your dwelling here.

Let the King behold your beauty,
Let his daughter shine
Above you all in cloth of gold
And needlework most fine!
O King, the richest rulers
Of the nations bow to you,
They race with one another
To find gracious deeds to do,

Bringing their most precious gifts,
Your favour to receive.
With joy and gladness they arrive,
And never wish to leave:
All the virtuous virgins,
All your daughter's royal friends,
All the royal sons as princes
To all lands God sends.

I will make your name, says God,
Remembered on the Earth
Forever and forever
With great praises, joy and mirth.

46

God is our sure refuge –
He who strengthens our defence.
He is always present,
Though great tumult stirs the seas.
Therefore we will have no fear
Though the air grows tense:
Though the mountains tremble
Like a petal on the breeze,

Though the Earth's depths reel and shake,
The waters rage and swell,
Though the ocean towers
In a torrent o'er our heads,
We will ride the river
On whose waters all is well,
Whose streams glide on in gladness
To the place our saviour treads:

To the Holy City,
To the house of the Most High;
God is in the midst of her
And she shall not be moved.
He will send to save her
When the morning light draws nigh;
Our great God is with us,
And His power shall be proved.

The nations are in uproar
And the kingdoms broken up,
But God need only say the word
And they shall melt away –
'Come and see', so calls us He
By whom we're taken up;
The God of Jacob is our stronghold
On the fateful day.

He has wrought destruction
On all those that would wage war;
He has ordered wars to cease
And snapped their spears as sticks;
He has broken all their bows,
Their weapons work no more;
All their armoured vehicles
His wrathful fire licks.

'Be still now,' is His word,
'And know that I am God on High.
I will be exalted
By all nations of the Earth.
I have ordered peace,
And who is there who dares defy?'
The Lord of hosts is with us:
Past all measure is His worth!

47

Clap your hands together,
Sing to God with shouts of joy!
All you peoples, now
Your greatest merriment employ!

For the Lord most High, He rules
Above the Earth as King,
He who all the nations
Under Israel's feet did bring.

He marked us out a heritage,
For Jacob, whom He loves;
He went up with merry noise,
The sound of singing doves.

Muster all your trumpets –
Sing your praises to our God;
Marshall all your skill and sing
Of Him who holds the rod

To rule above the nations,
Who is seated on His throne,
Whom all the peoples of the Earth
As God and King will own.

Abraham's proud children,
All the peoples flock to you,
All the mighty powers
And the nations' nobles too.

He is high exalted,
All the Earth belongs to Him,
And all her powers join in songs
That with great gladness brim!

48

God is great: His praises
Through His holy city sound,
The city where divinity
Upon the Earth is found.
Mount Zion is His holy mountain,
Fair and lifted high;
Where His mighty dwelling stands
And stretches to the sky.

He visited her palaces,
He ruled there as her king,
And showed himself with surety,
That refuge He would bring:
For lo, the kings of Earth assembled,
Eager to attack;
Greedily they swept upon us –
And He swept them back.

In their pride they came to conquer,
Multitudes they led;
But when they saw His splendour,
In dismay they turned and fled.
Utterly dumfounded
Were the rulers of the Earth;
In agony they writhèd
Like a woman giving birth.

Their limbs were seized with trembling,
By terror were they pinned,
Then scattered as when wooden ships
Are shattered by the wind.
It's just as we had heard of old:
This miracle we've seen,
That God with all His mighty host
Among us here has been,

And He has established us,
His city evermore –
We'd waited long to see
Your loving-kindness, Lord, before,
In your Holy Temple,
Built to testify to you;
Your right hand is full of justice,
Great deeds do you do!

And now the nations praise you
And your name rings round the Earth:
Now Mount Zion will rejoice
And Judah fill with mirth!
Because of your just judgements, Lord:
We see them all around,
Set firm as mighty towers here
Henceforth in Zion found.

Consider all her bulwarks,
And her mighty citadels:
That our God will be our guide
Forever, she foretells.

49

All that dwell throughout the world,
Come hearken to my word:
Lowly ones who labour,
And you wealthy lords alike –
Rich and poor together,
Hear what I myself have heard,
Mine ear inclined to parables,
To witness what is right.

My mouth shall speak with wisdom,
Many riddles I'll unfold,
I'll meditate on understanding,
Where I set my heart;
That all the peoples may perceive
This truth revealed of old,
I'll meld it into melody
By skilled musicians' art.

Why should I fear to speak my mind,
Though danger stalks my days?
Those that would destroy me
Rise in wrath on every side,
But frail is their fickle strength,
Who walk in wicked ways –
They glory in their goods,
And in abundance hope to hide.

They can't afford deliverance,
The ransom of their souls,
Though they gather all the gold
And silver in the Earth:
The sin of man is such
That he can never pay the toll,
And horded heaps of worldly wealth
To God are nothing worth.

Did they think that they could buy
Their bodies from the grave,
And could live for ever
On the basis of their gain?
See: though wise in winning wealth,
Themselves they cannot save;
With the poor and ignorant
They perish just the same.

The tomb will be their home eternal,
While the long years pass;
Others will divide the wealth
They struggled to accrue:
Wasted were their wicked lives,
Who sleep beneath the grass,
The lands they took in triumph lost,
By others named anew.

Many who have Earthly honour,
Boasting in their fame,
Who love to look upon themselves,
Delight in their own voice,

Have no understanding,
And will soon behold their shame,
For down into the pit descends
The path that is their choice.

Death will be their shepherd;
Like a flock of slaughtered sheep
Death will be their destiny,
Delighters in themselves,
When their beauty wastes away,
They will but watch and weep,
In dead and barren dwelling-places
Ever doomed to delve.

Do not fear, when some grow rich,
Whose glory waxes fat;
Who think themselves contented
And advise you gather wealth;
Empty are their praises,
For in death they will fall flat
And carry nothing with them
That they gathered for the self.

They, with their foul fathers,
Will sleep ever in the dark,
And perish like the ignorant
And base beasts that they are,
But God will ransom my poor soul,
For unto Him I hark;
From the grasping grave
He'll take and rescue me from far.

50

Hear the Lord, who's spoken,
Who has called the world to be;
Who makes the Sun to rise and set
Each day by His decree.

Perfect in His beauty,
God shines out from Zion's hills –
He will not keep silence,
For His voice the heavens fills!

Fire goes before Him
To consume what blocks His way:
A mighty tempest rages
That no scheme of man can stay.

He comes to judge the Earth,
And hold His people to account:
'Gather now the faithful ones
Unto my Holy mount –

'Those who in my covenant
With sacrifice are sealed.'
Heaven sings His righteousness,
Whose judgement is revealed.

'Hearken to my speech, my people:
I will testify.
I am God, your God,
And deeds of good and bad I'll try.

'The sacrifice you gave me
Was not pleasing to my sight:
Burnt offerings before my face
You proffered day and night,

'But I desire no flesh of bulls,
Nor he-goats that you kill:
Mine are all the living cattle,
Beasts on every hill.

'I know every single bird
Who on each mountain sings,
And every insect of the field,
The pattern of its wings;

'Mine the creatures of the forest,
Sky and ocean too:
If I hungered for their flesh,
Why would I tell you?

'Do you think I dine on bulls,
Or drink the blood of goats?
Who is this who slays my creatures,
Then before me gloats?

'Such slaughter is abomination:
Such sacrifice I hate;
An offering of thankfulness
Would better satiate.

'Give to God your thanks and praise,
Your vows of grace fulfil,
Call to me in time of trouble –
This is what I will.

'I will save you from distress
And you will honour me,
But to the wicked I proclaim:
Your double heart I see.

'Why do you speak empty words?
My statutes you recite,
You claim to know my laws,
And yet refuse to do what's right!

'You cast my Word behind you,
And you think I do not see
When with thieves you bargain,
To adulterers you flee

'And join with them in evil deeds,
Your lips so full of lies:
You sit and slander your own kin,
Your brother you despise.

'Did you think that I
Am even such a one as you?
That I would stay in silence
And ignore these things you do?

'No! I shall reprove you –
I shall set before your face
All the evil you have done,
Your record of disgrace.

'You who soon forget your God,
Consider this and learn,
Or I shall destroy you –
And to none else can you turn.

'You thought you could placate me
By your slaughtering of beasts –
But honour me with offerings of thanks,
Not bloody feasts!

'Give to me a sacrifice
Of faithfulness each day,
For I shall show salvation yet
To those who keep my way.'

51

O God, so great in goodness,
Please me merciful to me.
Wash me of the wickedness
I wrought unworthily.

Wellspring of compassion,
Clean away my foul misdeeds:
Cleanse me of the sin
That chokes my soul like thorny weeds.

I acknowledge all my faults,
My sin before me lies;
And I can see how ugly
I must be before your eyes.

I have cast off goodness,
And done evil in your sight;
You have found me wanting
And your judgement, Lord, is right.

Sentence me to painful death,
For I am nothing worth:
I have been a wicked sinner
Even from my birth.

From my first conception,
In my mother's womb, I erred;
Long ago of wisdom
And of goodness I despaired.

Yet you desire truth to dwell
   Within my deepest part –
   You dig wells of wisdom
   In the desert of my heart.

Purge me with your hyssop, Lord,
   And scrub my innards clean:
   Wash me of my wicked sin
   That snow white might I gleam.

Make me hear of joy and gladness,
   With a merry voice –
   Let this bag of broken bones
   Be mended and rejoice!

Turn your face from my foul sin
   And blot out my mistakes –
Cleanse my heart and make me clean,
   While good in me awakes!

From your gracious presence
   Do not throw me in disgust,
Nor take your Holy Spirit from me:
   You I long to trust.

Show again your saving help
   And give again your joy;
   Send again your Spirit
   And my soul do not destroy!

Then I will recite your ways
To wicked ones, and teach
Vile sinners like myself
That they may practice what you preach.

My lips shall sing of righteousness,
My mouth pour out your praise;
If only you instil my tongue
To speak a goodly phrase!

God, deliver me from guilt;
It drags me to the ground:
In your heart is no desire
For butchered creatures found,

Nor do you delight in flesh
That's offered up in fire;
A broken spirit is the sacrifice
That you desire.

Look upon my contrite heart,
My Lord, and hate me not;
Zion and Jerusalem, your own,
You've not forgot;

For when you build their walls up high
And there your house renew,
I shall dwell, a sacrifice of righteousness
To you.

52

O, you wicked tyrant!
In your tyranny you trust;
You delight in evil,
Whereas goodness you despise.
Know you not that God is He
Whose judgement will not rust?
Vain is your destructive plotting,
Your deceitful lies.

You like to utter falsehood,
And you spurn the Word of Truth;
You love to wound with words that hurt
And lead God's flock astray.
Therefore God will thrust you down:
Your fall will be the proof,
When He plucks you from your seat,
That fruitless is your way.

From amongst the living will He pull you,
Like a weed,
And all the righteous tremble
At your haughty pride's collapse;
Scornfully they'll laugh at you,
'See what becomes of greed!
This is he who let the love of God
Within him lapse!

'He trusted in his riches
And exalted in his wealth;
With the rod of wickedness
He beat the needy poor.
Yet for all his pompous strength
He cannot save himself –
Slaughtered by his own sharp tongue,
He gropes upon the floor!'

But I within the house of God
Shall set my root and grow,
Spreading like an olive-tree
Well-nurtured by His love;
I will thank the Lord
For all the goodness He did show,
And trust in you, O God,
With all the faithful ones above.

53

The fool has said within himself
That God does not exist,
That there is none to witness his
Corrupt and evil thoughts –
In abominations, wicked,
He does not desist,
Nor does he do any good
Who at God's wisdom snorts.

God has searched this generation,
Looking down in vain
To see if there is any
Who in wisdom seeks His will.
All alike have gone astray,
Gone seeking worldly gain;
He looks for righteous children
In mankind, and He finds nil.

Why, they are corrupted:
There is no one that does good –
They mop up God's own people
Like they would devour bread.
Have they then no knowledge?
Can they not have understood?
They call not on the Lord,
For see – they vaunt themselves instead.

But soon they will be trembling –
They will fall into great fear,
Such a fear as never was,
When they are put to shame.
For God will break and scatter
All the bones of those who jeer,
And cast off those who wedded sin
And would not heed His name.

O, that Israel's saviour
Would from Zion come, and soon;
That God would turn again the fortunes
Of His children sad:
Come, O come, our saviour:
Come, and with a merry tune
Jacob will rejoice again
And Israel be glad!

54

God, I beg you, hear my prayer
And look upon my plight:
You alone can save me,
And your power prove me right.

Heed the words I call to you,
For see, the ruthless rise;
Strangers seek to take my life,
And your name they despise.

Behold: my God will help me,
He alone upholds my life.
But evil will rebound on those
Whose wickedness is rife:

Destroy them through your mighty strength,
All those who lie in wait,
And I will praise your name, my God,
Whose gracious love is great.

A free heart do I offer you,
Who saved me 'midst my woes;
Gladly do I give it,
For the downfall of my foes.

55

Hear my prayer, O God.
Do not be deaf to my request.
Give heed to me, and answer:
in my pain I cannot rest.
I hear the wicked clamour,
And I call out in alarm:
Furious, my foes descend,
Intent to do me harm!

My heart, it is disquieted,
I feel the fear of death.
A pall of dread has fallen
And draws out my very breath.
I am overwhelmed, I tremble;
Terror strikes by day –
O that like the wingèd dove
I could but fly away!

Then would I make haste and flee
from storm and trial and test:
Then would I in distant places
lodge and find my rest.
Confuse their tongues, divide them up
who build their Babel towers!
I have seen their cities,
where such strife and hate devours.

Day and night they walk her walls,
with violence their wares;
Wickedness patrols her streets,
oppression stalks her squares.
It was not an open foe
That sought to cast me down –
Surely, I'd have hid from him
Who wears a wicked crown;

Then I could have borne it,
From the one whose guile I knew,
But O, my dearest friend – my close companion –
It was you.

Together we took counsel
As we walked in God's sweet place;
Then you smiled upon me,
Now such malice screws your face!
We were kindred fellows – you,
My own familiar friend,
Have stretched your hands against me;
All your pity was pretend.

Your speech was soft as butter,
Silken words that flowed like oil;
Now I see that all your heart
Was but to rob and spoil.
Your voice is cruel and heartless now,
Your words are naked swords;
But as for me, I look to God,
Who serves out just rewards.

Morning, noon and evening
I will sob my humble prayer,
And He will not abandon me;
He'll snatch me from the snare
And put my soul in peaceful places,
Rescued from the throng;
He will hear and bring them down
Who sought to do me wrong.

Let death descend upon them:
Throw them, living, to the Pit!
They are steeped in wickedness,
Their dwellings drenched in it!
Their souls are spoiled beyond redeem,
For they will not repent:
They have no fear of God
Until their wicked lives are spent.

Then they'll understand, O God –
They'll not live half their days
Before the blood they shed,
Their vain and cruel, deceitful ways,
Will fall upon their own heads –
God, my trust shall be in you,
Who will not let the righteous fall,
Whose love is just and true.

56

Have mercy on me, God:
My foes would tread me to the ground.
All day long in their assault
They press and hem me round.
Without end mine adversaries
Trample me in glee,
And many are the foes
Who make their haughty wars with me.

In the day of fear
I put my trust, O God, in you:
In God I trust and will not fear,
For what can mere flesh do?

All day long they wound me
With their words: their every thought
Devised to do me evil,
And great trouble have they wrought.
They lay in wait to slay me,
Watching every step of mine –
Shall they, for such wickedness,
Escape thy wrath divine?

You have counted all my groaning,
Stored up all my tears
In your bitter bottle:
In your book are writ my fears.

Rise up in your anger, Lord,
And cast the peoples down:
On the day I call to you
My foes will turn around
And shrink back from their evil,
Because God is on my side –
The God whose word I praise,
The Lord in whose help I abide.

In God I trust and will not fear,
For what can mere flesh do,
Since I draw protection,
O most gracious Lord, from you?

To you, O God, I will fulfil
The vows that I have made:
Offerings of thanks
Upon your altar I have laid,
For you will keep my soul from death,
My feet, they will not fall,
That I might walk alive
Before my God, the light of all.

57

Be merciful to me, my God,
Be merciful to me;
For my soul salvation finds,
And refuge, but in thee.
In the shadow of your wings
For safety I shall fly:
I hide in you until
The storm's destruction passes by.

God, who keeps His purpose for me,
He will send and save,
And rebuke the beasts
That all around me romp and rave.
Their teeth are fierce arrows
And their tongue a sharpened sword,
But God will send His faithfulness
And love as my reward.

They laid a net to trap me,
Sought to dig for me a pit:
My soul was pressed to death,
But they themselves will fall in it!
God above the heavens,
Whose great glory fills the Earth,
I shall sing and praise you
With the music of my mirth!

Rouse my soul with harp and lyre,
Liven up the dawn!
My heart is ready for my God
And no more do I mourn:
I will give you thanks, O God,
Among the peoples, praise;
Towards the height of Heaven
My great love for you I raise!

You are faithful to the clouds,
Your love the world is worth:
God above the heavens
Whose great glory fills the Earth!

58

You powerful, give heed:
You may be mighty, are you just?
Do you govern fairly
All the people in your trust?

No: devoid of justice
Are your deeds throughout the land;
With greed you sap your subjects
As you strike them with your hand.

The wicked, they have wandered
Far astray from at the first:
Even since they left the womb
Has falsehood been their thirst;

Venomous as vipers
And as poisonous as asps,
Deaf as is the striking adder
To its victims' gasps.

It does not heed the charmers,
Stops its ear to their spells,
Though skilfully they weave their nets,
Or loudly ring their bells.

Smash, O Lord, the sharpened teeth,
The fangs they bare to bite;
Let them be as dried up water,
Vanished out of sight!

Let them wither as the winter grass
Is trodden down;
Let these lions languish
Like the summer herb burnt brown;

Let their refuse vanish
Like the snail's slimy track –
Those wicked deeds and wrongs they wrought,
Never to come back!

Let them be like babes
Who die before they see the Sun!
Let the wares they make be smashed
Before their work is done!

Then the righteous will have gladness,
On that vengeful day,
Seeing all these machinations
Swiftly swept away!

They will bathe their feet in blood
Burst out of evil veins;
When the wicked all lie slain
They'll cry 'the Lord God reigns!

'Truly will the righteous
Have a harvest of great worth:
Truly God is with us,
Giving judgement on the Earth!'

59

O my God, I call out
For your rescue from my foes:
Set me high above the rising,
Raging flood of those –
Deliver me from all who muse
On murder, lying low
To pounce upon my simple soul
And deal a cruel blow!

Save me from these high and mighty
Evildoers all,
Who through no fault nor sin of mine
Are plotting for my fall:
Needing no excuses,
They prepare themselves for war,
But you are Lord of Hosts alone –
Have pity on the poor!

Rouse your strength,
See my foul foes and strike them for my sake!
Let your righteous judgement
On the nations now awake!
God, do not have mercy
On the treacherous and mean,
Who stalk the streets by night
To snatch their victims when unseen.

They prowl about the city
Like a snarling pack of dogs,
Evil words they whisper
As they eat us up like hogs –
Slashing swords are all their speech,
Designed to cut us deep,
'For nobody can hear us,'
They say, 'everyone's asleep.'

But you, O lord, will laugh at them
On hearing them on High:
You hold them in derision
When they make their boastful cry.
You, my God, are my strong wall;
Their words will not prevail –
I will watch and wait for God
Whose strength will never fail.

He will swoop and rescue me
In His abounding love,
He will lift me up
To see their downfall from above.
Lord, slay not my foes in case
My people all forget:
Bring them down instead,
Consume their conscience with regret!

Scatter all their boasted pomp,
My champion and my shield –
Let their sordid speech
And lying lips be now revealed!

Because of all the curses
And the falsehood that they spoke,
Let them be consumed in anger,
Let their pride be broke,
Let them know that God alone
Rules over Jacob's land:
All the ends of Earth are His,
All strength is in His hand.

Listen! They return again,
Still snarling in the night,
But every morning I will praise
Your steadfast love, your light.
You have been my refuge
Through the troubles of the day;
I sing to you, my strength
In whose firm stronghold I will stay.

60

O God, my God, you cast us off,
Your anger has been hot;
You have smashed and broken us
As an unwanted pot.

You shook the Earth and tore it up,
You pounded it with rain;
Heal its wounds – we tremble,
Bring us back to life again!

You have made your people
Swallow deep a bitter draught,
The deadly drink you've given
Makes us reel as on a raft,

Tossed upon the fierce tempest
Of an angry sea:
You have caused all those
Who fear your name to turn and flee.

They are shot by storms of arrows,
Flying from the bow –
Deliver your beloved,
For their desperate plight you know;

Save us by your mighty strength,
And answer us, we pray!
God in His great holiness
Of old was heard to say:

'I will triumph over Shechem,
Succoth I shall slice –
I will share his valley out,
Divide it in a trice.

'Gilead and Manasseh and Ephraim
Are mine,
Judah is my sceptre
To convey my strength divine.

'Moab, it will be my wash-pot –
I will rinse it out,
Edom will I crush,
Across Philistia I'll shout.'

Who, then, Lord, will lead me
Through the city's guarded gate?
Who will bring me into Edom,
Whose defence is great?

Have you not abandoned us,
And left up stripped of strength?
Will you not go forth
Amidst our troops again at length?

Give us help against our foe,
For Earthly help is vain –
We will do great deeds when you
Tread down our foes again!

61

Hear my crying, O my God:
Listen to my prayer.
From Earth's ends I call to you;
In Searching for you there

My heart is faint and weary now,
And desperate grows my cry;
I long for you to lift me up
Upon a mountain high.

You are there, my refuge,
My sure fortress and my tower,
Far above the troubled fray –
My foes there have no power.

Please let me for ever, Lord,
Be safe within your tent:
Safe beneath the shadow of your wings
I lie content.

You, O God, have heard my vows
And will grant my request;
You will give your king long life,
And days of peace and rest,

With his life enduring
While the generations pass:
May he sit enthroned with you,
Not withered like the grass.

Steadfast love surrounds him,
Truth watches him by night,
So day by day I praise you
As I ponder in delight!

62

On God my soul in stillness waits;
I hold my longing breath,
For He alone can save me
From the gaping brink of death.

God, He is the rock and stronghold
Upon which I stand;
I will not be shaken
At mine adversary's hand.

Why, they would destroy me
As they might a leaning wall –
They plot to push me over,
Like a tottering fence to fall;

They seek to thrust me down in shame
From this, mine honoured place:
With lies they would accuse me,
Have me cast off in disgrace.

In their mouths are honeyed words,
But in their heart they curse;
In God alone in stillness
I my wearied soul immerse.

Yet in Him I hope,
My rock that cannot be removed:
All my strength and glory is from Him,
Whose strength is proved.

God, my rock and refuge,
God my strength through all my days:
Pour your troubled hearts before Him,
Peoples, give Him praise!

All the nations are a whisper,
Passing like a sigh;
All man's vaunted vanities
Are but an empty lie.

On the scale they sit at naught,
More vacuous than air –
Put no trust in worldly wealth,
Nor trip upon its snare.

Take no pride, though riches grow,
Prosperity increase,
For this will count for nothing
At your hour of decease.

All that's good belongs to God –
I've often heard Him say
That He has every power:
He will keep you in the way.

Turn you not to tyranny,
Nor rob your neighbour's gain;
All who gather by oppression
Curse themselves in vain.

But steadfast love belongs to God –
On Him the good man feeds,
And He rewards both saint and sinner
For their Earthly deeds.

63

God, you are my God:
For you in eagerness I seek;
My very soul, it thirsts for you
As in a parchèd land.
My very flesh, it faints for you,
And I am very weak,
As in an empty desert
Where there's naught to drink but sand –

So I long to gaze on you
And on your Holy place;
As one who in a wilderness
Looks wearily for rest,
So would I behold your might,
The glory of your face,
For your great love, beyond my very life,
I love the best.

My lips, they long to praise you –
I will bless you while I live;
Mine arms, they stretch to heaven
As they yearn your feet to touch.
My soul shall be best satisfied
With all that you will give,
More than marrow fatness
That the belly craves too much.

My mouth shall sing with joy surpassing
All that Earth can yield;
I cling to you with all my soul,
For you will hold me tight;
On my bed I meditate
On all you have revealed,
And bring to mind your mercies
In the watches of the night.

You have been my helper;
In the shadow of your wings
I will rest rejoicing,
Safe from every prowling foe.
For some there are who seek my soul,
To bind me down with strings,
But those who would destroy me
To the depths of Earth will go:

You, God, will defend me,
You will slay them with the sword,
You will cast their carcases
For jackals to consume;
But your King and those
Who trust in you, you will reward,
And will stop the lying mouths:
Let silence be their doom.

64

Listen to my voice, O God –
In my complaint I call;
My life stands in jeopardy
And into fear I fall.

The enemy is hunting me,
The wicked ones conspire,
The evildoers gather
Like the flies around a fire.

They sharpen up their twisted tongues
Like one would do a sword,
They aim their wicked words like arrows,
Bitterly outpoured,

They shoot from secret places
Where they hide and are not seen,
They prey upon the blameless,
Striking suddenly and clean.

They hold fast to an evil course
From which they will not sway,
Setting up their traps and snares,
'For who will see?' they say.

So they look for cruelty,
And cunning is their ploy –
Deep within their inmost heart
They seek but to destroy.

But they shall see, when God's swift arrow
Shoots them from behind,
How quickly they are wounded,
With their deeds paid back in kind –

Those who sought to snare their neighbour,
Suddenly they fall,
Caught within the wicked web
Of their own words, and all

The people who pass by them
Wag their heads and spit with scorn –
All shall see what God has done,
A sign through which to warn.

They shall ponder all His works
And put their trust in Him;
The righteous shall rejoice,
The true of heart with praise shall brim!

65

To God, who answers every prayer,
All our praise is due.
Every living creature
Will confess our sins to you:
All our mountainous misdeeds,
You wash them all away,
Though they tower against us,
When to you our vows we pay.

Happy will be those you choose
To dwell within your courts,
Safe from death's destruction
Midst the blessings of your thoughts;
With wonders you will show us
Your salvation, hear our pleas
And shine your light through all the Earth
And to the farthest seas!

O hope of all creation,
By whose strength the hills were set,
Who stills the raging waters –
For your might cannot be met –
Who silences the roaring waves
And warring peoples calms,
The God who by His marvels
Every distant land alarms.

The great gates of the dawning day
　　And evening's dusk sing praise;
　Through the day you water us,
　　Who thanks in plenty raise.
　God's river bursts with water,
　　To replenish every turf:
　You provide your people grain,
　　Prepared for all the Earth.

　You drench the thirsty furrows
　And you make the ridges smooth:
　　So your soft, sweet showers
　　Blessings bring to every groove.
　Your paths are paved with plenty,
And your year with goodness crowned:
　　The pastures of the wilderness
　　With fresh fruit now abound.

　　Joy springs up across the hills,
　　The meadows thick with sheep,
　　The valleys sing with laughter
　　For the corn that stands so deep!

66

All the Earth, rejoice in God:
Sing glory to His name,
Sing glory to His praises
And His awesome deeds proclaim!

Because of your great strength, O God,
Your enemies will fall
And bow before their maker –
Earth shall worship, one and all.

They will sing your praises,
To behold the works of God
Who with mankind deals wondrously:
Their feet with faith He shod

And led them through the raging sea –
For Him it shrank away –
And across a river where
He held its flow at bay.

His hand rules for ever
In the splendour of His might;
All the nations slumber
Underneath His watchful sight.

None will rise against Him –
All the peoples praise the Lord,
Great the volume of the voices
Lifted in accord!

He who holds our slender souls
And keeps us yet in life,
He who sets our footing sure
And saves us in our strife,

He who proved us in the fire,
Our souls as silver tried,
Who left us in the snapping snare
In terror to abide,

Who broke our backs with heavy burdens,
Crushed us under foes,
Who brought us through both fire and water
When from death we rose,

And carried us to freedom
In a fair and pleasant place –
He we come to glorify
For all His loving grace!

I will come into His house
And offer there the fat:
I will make my sacrifices –
All I have at that –

And in sacrificial smoke
Will pay God what I vowed,
When amidst the storm of troubles
I cried out aloud.

Come and listen, one and all:
By my story hear
All that God has done for me,
All you who know His fear:

I cried out with all my might
And praised Him with my tongue,
And that very moment
Was my rescuing begun!

If I spoke with lying lips,
With evil in my heart,
The Lord would not have listened,
I would have been torn apart

By all that would oppress me –
Yet He heard my humble voice,
And in truth delivered me
For mercy is His choice.

Blessed be the Lord my God
Who did not spurn my prayer,
Nor withheld His love from one
Who longed that love to share!

67

God will give us His blessing,
He will fill us with His grace;
Like the shining Sun we see
The wonder of His face.

His way will be known in all the Earth,
His power be proclaimed,
And all the peoples praise our God,
'Midst all the nations named.

Let the nations all rejoice,
The peoples brim with mirth:
God will judge us justly
And will govern all the Earth.

O God, let peoples praise you,
Throughout all the Earth proclaimed,
Whence brims forth abundant fruit
By God's great love inflamed!

God, our God, will bless us
With much love and light and mirth,
Who from end to end is honoured
Over all the Earth!

68

Let God arise, for then
His foes will scatter to the wind:
They will flee who hate Him,
Who in spite of Him have sinned.

As smoke that billows
From the fire vanishes away,
So may they dissolve to nothing
On that awesome day.

As wax melts in the heat of flame
Their stern resolve will melt,
When they come before Him
And His presence they have felt.

Let the wicked perish,
Yet the righteous will be glad:
Before their Lord much merriness,
Rejoicing, will be had.

Sing to God: sing praises
To the One who rules the sky,
Rejoice to God:
This is His name, the Lord who rules on High!

Father of the fatherless,
And friend of the bereft,
Who brings the lonely home,
From whom no poor man's plight is left –

To His holy dwelling-place
He brings the captives free,
Leaving in the desert those
Who deal out misery.

God, you went before your people
In the desert waste;
The Earth, it shook beneath you –
By your presence was it faced;

The presence of the God of Israel,
Sinai's mighty Lord,
At your Word from heaven
Was a gracious rain outpoured.

You refreshed the thirsty land,
You slaked your people's thirst,
They settled down to dwell there
Where you'd planted them at first.

Lord, of your great goodness
You provided for the poor,
You sent forth the happy news
Of victory in war!

The women bore the tidings,
From their mouths came shouts of glee:
'We at home divide the spoil,
For kings and armies flee!'

Though you stayed to tend the sheep,
Look to the sky: behold!
A dove's wings dipped in silver,
And its feathers with green gold!

For the Lord Almighty
Scattered kings like flakes of snow:
All the mighty mountains gape
With envy in a row,

Looking to God's mountain
Where alone He chose to dwell;
Bashan's towering mountain
Looks in humble awe as well!

He will dwell forever there,
The Lord in holy power,
Whose chariots are countless thousands –
Why look on and cower?

He has led captivity,
A captive, from its throne;
He received the tribute
And returned to rule His own:

Even those who once rebelled,
Their burdens' weight He bears;
God is our salvation,
And His land no more despairs.

God alone, the mighty Lord,
Delivers us from death;
All His fierce enemies
Will feel His angry breath –

He will smite their hairy scalp
Who walk a wicked track,
He has said 'from Bashan's heights
I'll bring my people back.

'I will raise them up,
Though in the sea's dark depths they lie;
Till they dip their foot in blood
Of foes I've caused to die.

'Your dogs will eat their evil flesh
Until they are no more.'
Your glorious processions,
God and King, we do adore!

The singers and musicians
Make glad music in the way,
Walking in the midst of maidens
Who on timbrels play.

Your courageous company
Sing blessings to their God –
Bless the Lord, all you
Who out of Israel's fount were shod!

At the head is Benjamin,
The least of all the tribes;
Then the royal Judah
Where great joyfulness abides;

The princes then of Zebulun
And Naphtali proceed –
Send your strength to us, O God,
And bless this holy seed.

Make fast what you wrought in us,
For your great Temple's sake,
The jewel of Jerusalem,
Where you all tribute take:

Kings will kneel and grovel,
Bringing splendid gifts to you;
With your word you drive away
The wild and beastly too –

All the herds of bullish armies,
All the brutish hordes,
All those who delight in war –
The peoples and their lords –

All who lust for silver,
In your anger tread them down;
Let Egypt bring bronze vessels,
Ethiopia her crown.

Sing to God, all kingdoms
Of the Earth both far and near –
Lift your hands to God,
And let us merry music hear.

He rides high above the heavens,
In the ancient height:
He sends down His voice of thunder,
With the sound of might.

Recognise His power,
And His splendour in this land,
Whose power is above the clouds,
Who holds us in His hand.

How fearsome is His holy dwelling,
Terrible is He!
May the God of Israel
By His people blessed be!

69

Save me, God, for I am drowning
In the water flood;
I sink into the mire,
Find no foothold in the mud.
I struggle in the sweeping depths;
The waters reach my neck;
My throat is raw from crying,
I am like a sunken wreck.

Weary with my weeping,
My sore eyes grow dark and dim,
For I have looked so long for God
But had no help from Him.
Those who bear me hatred
Are as many as my hair;
They have no cause to hate me,
Yet they do so without care.

They accuse me falsely,
And I cannot match their might:
To give back what I never stole
To them cannot be right.
God, you know that I am foolish,
Find my every fault;
Let not those who trust in you
By me be made to halt.

Let not my example
Become their disgrace and shame;
My reproach has come
Because I trusted in your name.
I am so ashamed,
A stranger even to my kin;
My own mother's children
Have rejected me for sin.

They treat me as an alien
Because of my great zeal:
The scorn of those who scorn you
And your house I too must feel.
I humbled me with fasting,
To that they took offence;
I girded me with sackcloth,
Which they saw as evidence –

I became a byword
To those sitting in the gate,
Who sing their drunken songs
And murmur slanders full of hate.
Yet as for me, amidst all this
I make my prayer to you:
I wait upon your answer
At the time when it is due,

Falling on your mercy,
Your salvation holding tight:
O drag me from this stinking mire -
I have no strength to fight! -

Out of these deep waters,
From those baying for my blood.
Let the deep not swallow me,
Nor leave me to the flood!

Let me not be lost forever,
Sealed within the pit.
Turn to me your mercy,
And your goodness – brandish it.
Hide your fair face not away,
Be swift to answer me,
Help me in my trouble
And my sinking soul set free.

Mine enemies are many, Lord:
Deliver me with haste,
Knowing how reproach and shame
Have all but laid me waste.
This reproach I've borne for you
Has broken my poor heart,
I am full of heaviness –
I sought one to impart

A modicum of comfort,
Or of pity, there was none:
They gave me only gall to eat
And vinegar for fun.
Lay a trap to take them
At the table where they feast,
Let it be a snare to them,
Let their delight be ceased.

Let their eyes be blinded,
In the darkness let them grope,
Let them tremble to their very loins,
Devoid of hope;
Pour out indignation
Like a liquid vat of lead,
Let the heat of all your anger
Fall upon their head.

Let their homes be desolate,
Their camps be overtook;
See how they have persecuted
Him whom you have struck.
They seek to pile on sorrow
For the one whom you have nailed,
Lay the guilt on them,
Their plea for vindication failed.

Wipe their names from in the book
Of life and righteousness,
But by your great salvation
Save me from my wretchedness!
I am poor and needy,
And my misery is great,
Yet I praise the Lord my God
And songs of joy create:

I proclaim God's greatness
With my words of sacrifice –
These much more than offerings
Of oxen will suffice.
More than bulls with horns and hooves,
My gift will please the Lord;
You who seek Him, do not think
You'll garner no reward.

The humble will look on and see,
And their heart will be glad;
They shall live, for God looks down
With love on those made sad.
He listens to the needy,
From our prison hears us call –
Let Earth and sea and Heaven praise,
And what is in them all:

Praise the God who saves us,
Who our cities will rebuild,
Who ensures that Zion
With His people will be filled,
Inherited by all His servants'
Children in His care,
For everyone who loves His name
Will flock and prosper there.

70

God, make speed to save me:
Let your longed-for help make haste;
Turn back in confusion
Those who lay my life to waste.
Put them in disgrace
Who would do evil and defame;
Counter those who mock me, Lord,
And shower them in shame.

But let all those who love you sing,
Rejoicing, and be glad;
Let all those who seek
The Lord's salvation not be sad.
As for me, I am but poor
And wretched, and in need;
Come, O Lord, and quickly –
Come to help me when I plead.

You, our great deliverer,
The help on which we stay,
Come and save us quickly:
O my Lord, do not delay!

71

O Lord, I seek your refuge:
Let me not be put to shame;
Save me by your righteousness,
Deliver me from blame;
Hear me when I call to you
And set your servant free:
A stronghold and a fortress I can run to
Be for me.

Send out help to save me,
Be the rock on which I stand;
Reach forth and deliver me
From mine oppressor's hand,
From the grasp of wicked ones,
The evildoer's tongue:
You have been my confidence,
My hope since I was young.

I've leant on you since first
You drew me from my mother's womb;
From my birth I've praised you,
I will praise you to my tomb.
To many I'm a portent,
A discomfort and a curse;
But you, God, are my refuge:
Let your praises fill my verse!

My mouth will sing your glory
All day long – forsake me not,
Though old age may weary me,
And strength succumbs to rot.

Mine enemies are talking,
They take council in the night;
They lie in wait to take my life,
They say 'put him to flight:
No-one can deliver him –
Go snatch him where he stands!'
They say, 'God has forsaken him:
His life is in our hands!'

O God, do not delay:
Be not far from me in my woe;
My hope in you is constant,
More and more your praise I'll show.
Let those who would destroy me
Be disgraced and scorned for shame:
Those who would do evil
Find reproach besets their name.

My mouth of your salvation
Will be singing without end,
My tongue of all your righteousness
A constant message send –
I'll begin to tell
Of all the mighty works of God,
I'll recall the righteousness
In which your footsteps trod.

You taught me since this aged man was young,
And to this day
I tell of all your wondrous works:
Forsake me not, I pray,
When I am old and weak,
That I your great deeds may pronounce
And to generations yet to come
Your acts announce.

Your righteousness, it reaches
To the heavens and the clouds:
Who like you can do such deeds
Amidst our Earthly shrouds?
Great troubles and such tempests
You have shown me in my life,
But you will yet refresh me,
Lift me high above my strife!

Bring me from the depths of Earth,
The cavern of despair;
Put me in a place of honour,
Show me comfort there.

O my God, I praise you
On the lyre and the strings;
I thank you for your faithfulness,
My soul in gladness sings,
For you have redeemed me,
So I praise you all day long:
Ashamed and disgraced will be
All those who sought my wrong.

72

Lord, give the King good judgement,
　Lend him knowledge of your law,
　That he may govern righteously
　　And justly help the poor.

　May His hand defend them
And His mountains ring them round,
　His hills keep safe their children
And with prosperous peace resound:

　He'll crush the cruel oppressor,
　　But the needy ones exult;
　May His foes kneel down
And lick the dust for their foul fault.

　In His time may goodness bloom
　　And flourish on the Earth;
　Like the mown grass springing up
　　When rain restores the turf.

　　May he never perish,
Though the sun and moon grow dim;
　All the Earth from sea to sea
　　Will come and bow to him.

　They'll give him gold from Sheba,
　　Seba too will bring him gifts;
　Kings of Tarshish and the Isles –
　　Each one a tribute lifts,

Falling down before His feet
And blessing him with prayers,
Who cracks down on oppression
and rewards the soul that cares.

He will hear the crying poor,
Bring help to those in need;
He shall show them pity
And their hungry mouths shall feed.

He'll preserve their precious lives
And violence stamp out:
His name, while the Sun and Moon endure,
They'll gladly shout!

Grain will grow abundantly,
Stand thick upon the hills,
Every tree will flourish
And bear fruit that fields fills,

Like grass upon the meadows:
Every nation your name sings –
And blessed be the Lord,
The One who does such wondrous things!

73

God's love is great for Israel,
For all those whose heart is pure,
But I confess the envy
That I felt, a fool, before.
I slipped from off the righteous path,
And almost lost my way,
I in ignorance the part
Of brutish beasts did play:

The wicked and the proud
In such prosperity I found,
Their rich lives free of pain or plague,
Their bodies sleek and sound;
They came to no misfortune
Like the other folk I saw,
Though the cloak of violence
And the lace of pride they wore.

Sin seeps from deep within them,
From their loveless hearts it flows;
They scoff, and speak with evil words;
They say 'how should God know?'
They count Him an oppressor,
He who watches from on high;
They curse the highest heaven
And with wicked words they lie.

So the people turn to them:
They find in them no fault,
While at ease they grow in wealth
And their own selves exult.
Was it vain I cleansed my heart,
While these saw such success?
I washed my hands in innocence,
I used my tongue to bless,

But every day you chastened me,
You struck me all day long –
Yet if I boast and curse as they,
I'll do your children wrong.
For a time I thought to understand,
But I could not,
Until I entered your embrace,
And saw the end they got:

You slipped them up in their high places,
Suddenly they fell
Down into destruction,
To the open mouth of hell;
They dally in delicious dreams
And act as if you sleep,
But they when you arise
Will wake to ever mourn and weep.

Embittered by my envy,
I felt pierced to the quick –
But now I see the truth,
My bad behaviour makes me sick.

I am always with you;
You will hold me by the hand,
And afterwards receive me
To the glory where you stand.

Who have I in heaven
To account to, Lord, but you?
What is there on Earth
That I would rather gain or do,
Than to draw more nearly
To the God who is my all?
Though my heart and flesh may fail,
Your love will never fall.

The fool who would forsake you
Sleeps for ever in the dust,
But God's great works I'll ever tell,
For in your hand I trust.

74

God, why have you disowned us –
Why scorch us with your wrath?
You ransomed us of old –
Why now completely cast us off?
We are your sheep: you purchased us
To shelter us from harm,
But now the wolves attack us and
You yet hold back your arm!

Hasten to the city,
And behold the endless waste:
Your sanctuary in ruins,
And defiled your holy place;
Your adversaries roared with hate,
They smashed your temple down,
Like axemen felling trees they brought
Her pillars to the ground.

They came upon her carved designs
With hatchets and with blows,
And set up foreign banners
In the place that you once chose.
They set ablaze your holy house,
They razed it to the ground,
They went about the land
And burnt all holy sites they found.

They said, 'why not make havoc?
Let us stamp this people out.'
They murdered all your prophets,
So that none remain to shout
Or show us signs and help us see
How long this pain will last –
Will you let this blasphemy
Go on till we are past?

Yet you are our God and King,
Who did such mighty deeds:
You split the sea to save us,
Drowned our cruel pursuers' steeds;
You crushed the mighty enemy,
You fed their flesh to beasts,
You cleft the rock that fountains flowed,
You set for us a feast.

You dried up ancient rivers
That we might pass safely through:
Yours the day and yours the night,
Yours spring and winter too;
The Moon and Sun were stablished,
And Earth's wide bounds, by your hand;
Do not let your people perish,
Whom you gave this land!

Remember how the foolish scoffed
And mocked your holy name,
Forget not now your humble people,
Lay us not the blame.
Look on your creation: see,
The Earth is dark and black,
Full of dens of violence –
Turn not to us your back!

We are poor and needy,
Yet we praise your name in hope:
Rise and cast our cruel oppressors
Down the endless slope!
Hear the chafing clamour
Of their violence and war,
Their tumult never ceases,
They revile you as they roar!

75

God, to you we give great thanks,
    Because your name is near:
We thank you that you come to us,
    As all your deeds make clear.

'I will take this chosen time
    To make my judgement known,'
You tell us, 'and with equity
    Will judge the Earth I own.

'Though it shakes and trembles,
    All its peoples tossed about,
I am He that holds its pillars steady,
    Strong and stout.

'Cease your baseless boasting,
    You who vainly vaunt yourselves!
Let him drop his haughty horns,
    Who into evil delves –

'Lay aside your mocking horn,
    Which wickedly you raise,
And stop your stiff-necked speech
Through which your own foul deeds you praise.'

Neither with the eastern dawn,
    Nor from the weary west,
Nor from the wilderness between
    Arrives our long-sought rest –

God alone will put one down
And raise another high,
Who alone is judge of all
And brings His justice nigh.

In His hand there is a cup,
A well-mixed wine of wrath,
A bitter drink and foaming,
Gathered in a giant bath;

The wicked He will make to drink it,
Pour it down their throats,
Until they've drained the very dregs,
All poisoned by their gloats.

But I will be forever
Making music to my Lord;
With the God of Jacob
I'll rejoice in my reward:
Instruments of evil
I will swiftly drop and break,
Lifting high the righteous horn
For my great saviour's sake!

76

God is known in Judah,
And His name in Israel heard;
To place His house in Salem
And in Zion He preferred.

There He broke both bow and arrows,
Smashed both sword and spear;
There in blinding, splendid light
Did God himself appear.

He ruined all the weapons
That they'd gathered up for war;
The boastful, stripped and plundered,
Were not boasting any more;

The proud were startled in their sleep,
The warriors were dead;
Neither horse nor driver dares
To lift his haughty head.

O God, when you are angry,
Who can stand before your face?
Your glory from the mountains shines
To show up our disgrace:

Your majesty is terrible,
Earth trembles and is stilled
When your voice of judgement breaks
And heaven's height is filled.

You arose to judge the Earth,
To save the lowly meek,
To crush the wrathful peoples
And to help the poor and weak.

Earth's kings, once great and lofty,
In their terror turn and flee;
Proud princes lose their spirit
When your might and power they see!

Make a vow of faith to God,
Your Lord, and keep it too:
Let all about bring gifts
To Him to whom all praise is due.

77

With weeping eyes I cry to God,
To God aloud I wail,
For God I know will hear me
Though all other helpers fail.
In the day of trouble,
In the night-time of distress,
My hand is stretched to God alone,
For I can find no rest.

My soul refuses comfort,
And my heart and spirit sink –
On God I ponder and I groan,
I cannot sleep, nor think:
Mine eyelids cannot close,
I can no consolation reach;
I stand so deep in trouble
That I cannot render speech.

When I muse on days of old,
Remember years long past,
To think how strength and happiness
Have fled, I am aghast.
With my heart I whisper
In the dead dark of the night
And search for understanding;
It is fled far from my sight.

Will the Lord reject us,
Cast us off for evermore?
Was our sin so great that He
Has shut for good the door?
Has His favour shrivelled up,
His mercy clean forgot?
Is His promise voided –
Will He leave us here to rot?
Where is now God's graciousness?
Is it shut away?
Why has His compassion
And good pleasure fled our day?

So I said, 'I grieve because
God's mighty strength has gone:
His right hand, His mighty arm
That once we rested on.'
I recall your wondrous deeds, O God,
You wrought of old;
I will ponder all your mighty acts
Of which we're told.

Your way, O God, is holy:
Who can be so great as you?
You delivered Jacob's seed,
Saved Joseph's children too.
You showed forth your power
Midst the peoples of the Earth:
You flummoxed them with wonders
And you proved to us your worth!

The waters saw you, God,
And they recoilèd back in fear;
The very depths were shaken up
On seeing you appear;
The clouds were burst asunder,
And the skies with thunder smashed;
Your arrows sped about our head
As forks of lightning flashed;

Your voice boomed through a whirlwind
And the very Earth did shake:
As you walked, the very sea
Was parted in your wake.
Though your steps could not be seen,
You led us through the deep,
And by the hand of Moses
Kept us shepherded, your sheep.

78

Hear this teaching, all my people:
Mark you well my word;
I shall tell a parable
Most worthy to be heard.

I shall speak a mystery
That we have known of old,
A story for all generations,
As our fathers told.

We'll not seek to hide it
From the children yet to come:
We shall sing God's praises,
And the wonders He has done.

Solemnly He laid a charge,
He made it Israel's law,
To teach their children all
That He with might had done before,

That the generations yet unborn
Might understand
And pass it on in turn to their own children:
God's command.

Then they'd put their trust in God
And not forget His deeds;
Then they'd know to keep
All His commandments and decrees,

Quite unlike their forebears,
Who so stubbornly rebelled,
Whose spirit was not set on God,
Whose hearts on Him weren't held.

The warriors of Ephraim,
He armed them with the bow;
They turned back from battle –
They were too afraid to go;

They didn't keep His covenant,
They trampled on His law,
They forgot the deeds and wonders
He had wrought before.

He did such great marvels
For their fathers in their plight:
He brought them out of Egypt,
Had the sea part at their sight,

He made the waters stand and halt,
Amidst the roaring sea,
He led them by a cloudy pillar
Where they might be free;

He sent a blaze of fire by night
And led them through the day,
He split the desert rocks
To give them drink beside the way;

He brought out streams from solid rocks:
Like rivers did they flow.
Yet how did they repay Him?
In His way they would not go.

They defied the Lord most High,
Within the desert waste;
In their hearts they tested Him
When food they sought to taste:

Speaking out against Him,
They said 'can God feed us here?
Yes, He struck the rock indeed
And made our drink appear –

'But can He give His people bread,
Or yet provide them meat?'
When the Lord heard this,
His fierce anger was complete.

His wrath was kindled against Jacob
Like a flaming fire,
For they put no faith in God
And thus aroused His ire.

How could they not trust Him,
Who had shown to them such love?
So He opened heaven's gates
And burst the clouds above:

He rained upon them manna,
Food of heaven, for their grain;
Mortals ate the bread of angels
On that empty plain.

He bade the east wind blow
And brought the south wind by His might;
He sent down flesh as thick as dust
That covered all their sight;

It fell amidst their camp
Like so much sand beneath the sea,
All around their tents,
So they consumed it greedily.

Yet their craving did not cease –
The food yet on their tongue,
God's anger rose against them
And destroyed the strong and young.

He did such wondrous works
That should inspire faith and awe,
Yet for all He did for them
They went and sinned still more.

So, in sudden terror
To an end He brought their days;
Like a breath their years were gone,
Foreshortened by their ways.

When He slew them, they would seek Him:
Earnestly they sought;
Repenting of their wickedness
They back to God were brought,

Remembering He was their rock,
Redeemer God most High,
Yet they did but flatter:
With their tongue they told a lie.

They had not returned to Him
Forever in their heart:
Faithless to His covenant,
From Him they'd quickly part.

But He was so merciful
That He did not destroy:
Turning back from wrath,
His own displeasure He'd alloy.

He forgave their wrongful deeds:
He knew they were but dust,
Passing, never to return,
Then vanished like a gust.

~~

How often in the wilderness
His people did rebel!
Many times within the desert,
Grieving Him as well –

So their God, the Holy One
Of Israel they provoked:
They did not recall the day
That He such might invoked

Against the fierce enemy,
And great redemption sealed;
How He brought them out of Egypt,
Out of Zoan's field;

How He turned the rivers
Of that nation into blood,
How its people thirsted,
Israel had not understood.

God sent flies to Egypt
Which devoured flesh and food,
He sent frogs which tipped the nation
To decrepitude,

He gave all of their produce
To the locust and the worm,
The caterpillar did consume
What they worked hard to earn.

He destroyed all Egypt's vines
And sycamores with hail;
He caused their flocks
And all their herds of cattle thus to fail;

He sent down His thunderbolts
And stoned them all to death,
Deadly angels flying out
From His destroying breath.

He let loose such blazing anger,
Fury burnt His path;
He spared not their very soul
In His unrivalled wrath;

He gave them to the pestilence,
All firstborn sons He slew:
Unto death all Egypt's fruit
And flower thus He threw.

He did all this that He might lead
His people out as sheep;
Like a flock He guided them
Across the mountains steep.

He led them into safety
And He conquered all their fear;
In the sea their enemies
Were made to disappear.

He brought them to His Holy place,
The mountain He possessed;
He drove out other nations
That they there might safely rest;

He shared out their inheritance,
To Israel's tribes their lot,
Yet all this He did for them
They straight away forgot!

Still they tested God most High,
Rebelled against His word,
Kept not His commandments
As if all this they'd not heard.

Like an arrow from a faulty bow,
They sprang aside;
Like their thankless forebears
They did not in God abide.

They slighted Him for idols,
Like the nations He threw out;
On the hills they set up altars,
Wickedness they'd spout.

When God had heard all they had done
His anger waxed strong:
He utterly rejected Israel
For their grievous wrong,

He forsook His tabernacle,
Left His Holy tent,
And His empty arc
Into captivity He sent.

He gave up all His splendour
For the enemy to take,
In His rage His chosen people
All did He forsake.

He let the sword destroy them,
Let the fire eat their young,
No-one left to mourn their maidens:
Not a song was sung.

Their priests were butchered by the sword,
Their widows could not cry,
For it seemed that everyone
Was surely then to die.

Then the Lord arose,
As when a warrior is roused –
He struck against the enemy,
Who violence espoused;

Not by Joseph's tribe,
Not Ephraim did He the same,
But chose the tribe of Judah
To bring all our foes to shame.

There He built His sanctuary,
On His holy hill,
Like the height of heaven there
His glory He'd instil.

So He chose His servant David
As His people's king:
From the ewes and rams
Within the sheepfolds him did bring,

That he might shepherd Israel
With a true, devoted heart,
And with a skilful hand
He did God's guidance there impart.

79

O God, the heathen came upon us,
Smashed your Temple door,
Reduced its walls to rubble
And defiled its holy floor.
Ruined is Jerusalem,
Your heritage a heap;
Your servants lie a slaughtered mass,
The few survivors weep.

The flesh of all your faithful ones
Is eaten up by beasts;
The circling birds pick pieces
From our unburied deceased.
We have no men to bury them,
So few now are we left:
Their blood flows out like water
All around – we are bereft!

How long, Lord, must your anger linger?
Look on our distress!
Your jealous fury burns as fire;
Our nation is a mess!
Pour your indignation
On the people who care not,
The kingdoms who know not your name
And your decrees forgot.

They devoured Jacob
Like a lamb before a wolf;
They destroyed His dwelling-place
And left a gaping gulf.

Do not hold against us
All our former stupid sin –
Come to us in your compassion,
Bring your people in.

For we are brought to great distress,
Our spirits very low:
Be our swift salvation,
For your gracious name we know.
Wash our sins away from us
And help us for your sake –
Why allow the heathen
To believe our faith is fake?

'Where is now their God?' they'll say,
'He has no strength to save!'
Let those nations know your vengeance
For the blood they crave.
Pity us, poor prisoners;
Your slaughtered servants see,
Hear our sighs of sorrow
And come, set your people free!

By your mighty arm and strength,
Release those doomed to die;
Turn the taunts our neighbours jeered
On them – their bitter cry:
Let the shame they meted out
Fall on them seven-fold;
For we, your cherished people,
Were your chosen flock of old.

Save us, God, for we
Will give you thanks for ever more
And through all generations
Tell your praise and mercy sure!

80

Hear your sheep, O Israel's shepherd.
We were once your flock,
When Joseph's children you led out:
our saviour and our rock.
Summon now your mighty strength
and help us in our need:
Turn us by your glorious light;
your sheep to safety lead.

God, will you be angry always,
shun your people's prayer,
And leave us only tears to drink,
and grief for bread to share?
You've made us but a laughing stock,
derision poured on scorn:
Our root and stem is broken down,
by savage beasts we're torn.

You planted us, a precious vine,
From Egypt brought with care,
And drove out other nations
That it might dwell safely there.
It rooted firm and flourished,
Stretched its branches to the sea;
It overshadowed every hill,
It topped the tallest tree!

Why, then, are its branches broken,
Battered to the floor?
All who pass by pluck its fruit,
They pillage all your store;
All the insects from the field
Devour what is left –
Look, and see our foes' fell deeds
And leave us not bereft!

Cherish now this precious plant
You nurtured for your own,
Salvage this surviving branch
That by your strength was grown.
Let those who cut its forest down,
Who burnt it with their fire,
Perish in the blazing heat
Of your consuming ire!

Let your hand of guidance
Lie upon him at your right,
The Son of Man you made so strong
To demonstrate your might;
And turn us by your glorious light,
Bright shining from your face:
Give us life and never
Will we cease your paths to chase!

81

Sing merrily to God,
O house of Jacob, sing with glee!
Sing with lyre and timbrel,
On the harp make melody!

At the new moon blow the trumpet,
At the full moon too,
As upon the special day,
The yearly feast, we do.

This will be a law of God,
For all Israel to keep:
The charge He set for Joseph's people,
Whom He led like sheep,

Out of Egypt's slavery:
A strange voice did I hear
Who said, 'I made the burden
On their shoulders disappear;

'Their hands that held such heavy loads
I loosened and set free;
I saved you from your trouble
When you cried for help to me,

'I answered you with mighty thunder,
High above the sky,
I proved your faith at Meribah –
Again I heard your cry –

'And now I will admonish you,
My people, hear my voice:
Let no strange or foreign god
Among you be your choice –

'Do not bow nor worship them;
I am the Lord your God,
Who brought you out of Egypt
And by whose safe steps you trod.

'Open up your mouths
And I shall fill them with much good.'
But my people would not hear;
They had not understood.

They would not obey me,
In the hardness of their heart;
So I sent them off
Upon their own paths to embark.

They clung to their own counsels,
Wouldn't walk within my ways;
O that they would heed my words!
I'd keep them all their days;

I'd soon see off their enemies,
Against such turn my hand,
And those who hate the Lord
Before His greatness would not stand.

They would be forever punished,
Humbled at my sight,
All of Israel's adversaries
Conquered by my might.

But Israel would I nourish,
On the finest wheat they'd feed;
With honey dripping from the rock
I'd satisfy their need.

82

God has called a council,
He in heaven takes His stand:
Amidst the gods He passes judgement;
Hear His reprimand –

'What is this I see?
You judge unjustly, favour wrong,
Condone the wicked actions of the wealthy –
For how long?

'You were to bring justice
To the weak and those in need,
To defend the orphan,
And the humble man to feed,

'To preserve the poor,
To keep the wicked from the weak:
Why, then, do you side with those
Who of oppression reek?

'They possess no knowledge:
See, they stumble in the dark;
They will not know wisdom,
But on mischief they embark.

'The very Earth's foundations shake
To such perversions see,
So I say, you may be gods –
My children you may be –

Yet as mortals nonetheless,
I tell you, you shall die;
Like one of these, their pompous princes,
Fallen you shall lie.'

Arise, O God, and judge the Earth,
For you alone are true:
He who shall possess all nations
Of the world, is you.

83

Lord, do not keep silence;
Do not hold your peace, O God.
Do not be unmoved: spare not
To raise your righteous rod.

See, our enemies that hate you
Lift their heads up high;
They scheme against your people,
Taking counsel on the sly.

They cook up a wicked scheme
Against your treasured race,
They say 'let's destroy them,
Let this nation be erased,

'That the name of Israel
May wholly be forgot.'
So in their conspiracy
With one accord they plot.

Edom and the Ishmaelites
Are members of their league,
Moab and the Hagarenes
Join in with their intrigue,

Ammon, Amalek and Ashur
Act like Zeeb, Zebar,
Zalmunna and Oreb,
Jabin, Midian, Sisera,

Whom you slew at Endor
To be dung upon the ground –
So let the commanders of these
Wicked tribes be found.

Philistia and those in Tyre
Gang against us too,
Strengthening the sons of Lot
Who give no thought to you.

All who say, 'let us possess
These pastures for our own' –
The pastures of our God –
Let them as thistledown be blown,

Chaff before the wind,
Or like the forest to a fire:
Let them be consumed
By the great flames of your fierce ire!

Let them burn like mountains
That in drought are set ablaze,
Let your tempest drive them
Like a madman in a craze,

Let your storm of wrath dismay them,
Cover them with shame,
That they turn back and repent
And come to seek your name.

For their evil let them be
Forever more disgraced;
Put them in confusion,
Let their rulers be abased.

Let them perish in their anguish:
They shall know that you,
Over all the Earth Most High,
Alone are Lord and true.

84

How lovely is that place, O Lord of hosts,
In which you dwell!
I long with all my heart and soul
To enter there as well.
For you my flesh rejoices all,
My heart, it sings aloud –
But those who dwell within your house,
They are the blessed crowd,

Whose strength they draw from you in life,
And praise you ever more;
Whose hearts are set on highways
Heading straight to Zion's door;
Who when they pass through barren valleys
Find therein a spring,
And early rains will fall to freshen
Those who call you King.

They will go from strength to strength,
Striding to your gates
To stand before our God
Who for the righteous pilgrim waits.
O God of hosts, hear my petition –
Jacob's God, give ear –
Be our sure defender,
See your children's faces here.

I'd rather live a day with you
Than years spent apart,
For you are both my sun and shield:
On you I've set my heart.
No good thing will God withhold
From those who walk with Him;
Blessed are the people, God,
Who with your mercy brim.

85

It was you, O God,
Who poured such grace on Jacob's woes;
Raised him from misfortune,
Rescued him from all his foes;
Forgave your pleading people
The offence of their great sin;
Laid aside your fury
And your fierce wrath reigned in.

Restore again, O God, your people:
Let your anger cease;
Surely not for ever
Your displeasure must increase.
Have pity on your people
As the generations pass,
Let your mercy give us life
Like rain on parchèd grass.

I will listen to the Lord
And in His words abide;
He shall teach us peace
That we no more may fall aside.
Truly, to the ones who love Him
Is salvation near:
That glory in our land may dwell,
We bow in reverent fear.

Truth and mercy meet together,

Righteousness and peace,
All kissing one another,
Whose embrace will never cease.
Truth is springing from the Earth
While righteousness smiles down:
From heaven God gives all that's good,
Exalted in renown.
Our land will yield its increase
Of the fruit that He has sown,
And righteousness direct His steps
When He to us is shown.

86

Listen, Lord, and answer me,
For I am in great misery.
I am poor, of no account,
And have no other help.
I have put my trust in you –
I have served you faithfully;
Save my soul, preserve me
When, a helpless dog, I yelp.

I have called you all day long –
Lord, make your mercy known;
Gladden now your servant,
For I am sore depressed.
I lift up my soul to you,
I call to you alone;
I know that you will answer
When I look to you for rest.

You are all forgiveness;
Love and goodness from your hand
Overflow to answer prayers:
There is none like you.
Neither god nor man could match
The works that you command;
Every nation of the Earth
Will glorify you too.

They will come and worship,
They will bow before your power;
Teach my feet to walk your ways,
My mind to know your truth;
Draw my heart to yours,
A comfort in my darkest hour,
And I will pour it out in thanks:
My shelter is your roof.

You have drawn me up again,
Saved from the gaping grave;
You have shown such steadfast love
And rescued my lost soul;
O God, preserve my life
For now the ruthless rant and rave –
The proud who do not look to you
Set evil as their goal.

You are slow to kindle anger,
Quick to light with grace;
You are full of kindness:
Turn your mercy now on me!
Give me strength to fight for you,
And save your poor son's face;
Show your favour's token
That the proud may shamèd be.

87

His foundation stands
Upon His holy mountain high:
God the gates of Zion loves
Above all others nigh.
Glorious things are spoken
Of the city of our God:
Every nation had her birth
In Zion where He trod.

Egypt, Ethiopia
And Babylon all know,
Philistia and Tyre too,
That this is where they grow,
And as they dance their tongues shall sing
What God was pleased to do:
'O Zion, source of all my springs,
The Lord has chosen you.'

88

O God, all day, and every night,
All I do is cry.
On my knees I plead before you:
Hear my humble prayer.
My soul is soaked in troubles,
For my life draws near to die;
I stray into the land of death –
O hear my crying there!

I languish, lost in darkness
Midst the pathways of the dead,
Amongst the tombs of those long slain
Whom you recall no more,
Cut off from your hand, your help,
And drowned in endless dread;
No strength now is left me,
Washed up on this woeful shore.

You dropped me in this dark abyss, Lord,
Threw me in the pit –
Your anger's heat so heavy
Presses down in crushing waves,
You've locked me fast in prison;
All alone in tears I sit,
My former friends abhor me now,
Or lie in silent graves.

My crying eyes have failed me, Lord:
You are my only help.
Day and night I call upon you,
Stretching out my hands!
God why have you rejected me,
A sorry, wretched whelp?
I only, morning, noon and evening,
Praise you in these lands –

These fields of foul destruction
Where your wonders are not known,
Where not a word of praise for you
Sounds from the lifeless shades,
Where dead men drown in darkness,
Since your name they will not own,
No light to show your faithfulness
Where dark despair invades.

All your lovingkindness
Is forgotten, and your deeds;
Like a flood of water
Do your horrors hedge me round
And close me in on every side:
My stricken spirit pleads;
God, why do you hide your face,
Nor hearken to the sound?

Since my wicked youth
I have been wretched unto death;
Now your terrors cloak me,
There is none to see my plight.

Yet still, O God, I call to you
With my last, gasping breath –
All who loved me have you hid,
And put my friends to flight.

89

My song I shall be always singing,
Throughout all my days,
Of the love and kindness of the Lord
In all His ways –

My mouth shall flow with praises
And your faithfulness proclaim,
To me and to all generations
Near and far, the same.

You stand as firm as heaven's dome,
Static as the stars:
As year by year the seasons pass,
Your love is always ours.

For you said, 'to David
I will make my promise sure,
My covenant establishing
His seed for ever more,

'That through all generations
They will not remove his throne.'
Earth and Heaven praise
Your wondrous works, Lord – yours alone –

And your steadfast faithfulness:
Your words will never fail;
Beside you all the hosts of heaven
Dim away and pale.

You, God, shall be feared
Amongst the holy ones on high:
You are great and terrible,
Above the clouds and sky.

Who is like to you, O God,
Your faithfulness a sea:
You command the raging waves
And bid the waters be.

Your enemies you dashed in pieces
With an outstretched arm:
Rahab crushed against the rock,
Who would have done us harm.

Yours are all the heavens' deeps,
And Earth's four corners too:
You established all the world,
It's creatures came from you;

You created North and South,
Made after and before,
Yours is a most mighty arm,
Your right hand strong in war.

Under your just government,
The mountains may rejoice;
On righteousness your throne is founded,
Faithful is your voice;

Love proceeds ahead of you
And happiness behind;
In your radiant countenance
We light and triumph find,

Resounding with our joy all day
To walk before your face,
Lifted up by goodness
From the shadows of disgrace.

You, our strength and glory,
In your favour lift our head:
Holy One, both Lord and shield,
The King whom evils dread!

~~

Long ago you spoke, Lord –
In a vision you appeared,
And said, 'I set a youth
Above the mighty to be feared;

'I have set a young man
Over all my people loyal –
David is my servant,
Now anointed with mine oil.

'I have found him faithful,
And my hand shall hold him fast,
Mine arm shall be his strength
Against the tempest's stormy blast;

'No enemy shall in their vain deceits
    With him succeed,
  Nor any evil one afflict
    In hatred, pride or greed:

'I will strike the foes that vex him
    Down before his face;
  I will beat down all who come
    Against him in disgrace.

'My Truth and love will be his blessing
    Throughout all his days;
  He shall be exalted
    For the sake of my name's praise.

'His dominion will stretch far
    Beyond the farthest sea;
  He shall rule the rivers,
    And shall ever call to me,

'"You are my great Father,
    And the rock on which I stand."
  He will be my firstborn,
    Beyond every king's command:

'The love I promised to him
    I shall keep for ever more;
  My command eternal
    Will stand fast with him for sure.

'His seed shall continue,
And his throne outlive the stars –
All the kings of Earth shall bow,
For nothing him debars.

'But if his children turn elsewhere,
Forget to keep my laws,
Lay aside my righteous judgements
And my goodly cause,

'Break my loving statutes,
Pay no heed to my commands,
I will scourge them for the sin
Committed at their hands.

'I will not withdraw my love,
Nor let my truth go dim;
I will not forget about
My covenant with him;

'Nor will I go back upon
The words which I have sworn,
Never to be false to him
Nor leave his sons forlorn:

'David's line shall dwell for ever,
As the ages run;
I shall set his throne before me,
Shining as the sun;

'It shall stand as long as light
Yet shimmers from the Moon,
My enduring witness,
Which will not be fading soon.'

~~

Yet now, Lord, you have cast us off;
Your chosen one is spurned:
His walls are smashed and broken down,
His precious city burned.

The covenant you forged with him
For ever, now you've broke;
His stronghold lies in ruins
Like the promise that you spoke.

Your anger raged against him
As you knocked his kingdom down;
Into dust and ashes
You have cast his mangled crown.

His precious store is plundered
By all they who pass him by,
His enemies exalted
And his foes all lifted high.

All his neighbours spit on him,
Cursing him with scorn;
Those who hate him sing for joy,
And he is left forlorn.

When he went to battle
You turned back the sword he swung;
Nor did you uphold him,
And his strength of arms you wrung.

His radiance no longer shines,
His guiding light is dark,
His throne is cast upon the floor,
His countenance is stark.

He was lately planted,
But you soon cut short his youth.
You have covered him in shame
To dare to trust your truth:

Lord, must you so utterly
Abandon us and hide?
How long shall your fiery anger
Yet with us abide?

Remember how my life is short,
How frail is my flesh:
There is no-one living that cruel death
Will not enmesh.

Who among this mortal race
Can cancel their demise?
Who can save their sinking soul
When deathly waters rise?

Where, Lord, is the steadfast love
You promised us of old?
Once you swore to David –
Now his people have been sold!

See how my foe scorns your servant,
Scarred by many taunts,
Always he derides me
And his hate for you he vaunts:

Do not let him slander
Your anointed steps again –
Blessed be the Lord for ever!
Amen and Amen.

90

O God, while generations pass
You are our constant guide:
Before the ancient mountains,
Everlasting you abide.
You made the Earth; you fashioned man,
And turn us back to dust;
You tell us, 'O my children,
Turn and give to me your trust'.

A thousand years, an age to us,
To you are but a day;
Our time, to you it passes
Like a nightly watch away.
You sweep away millennia
As if a passing dream,
Like the grass that flourishes
Then shrivels up they seem.

In your sore displeasure
We in vain consume away,
At your indignation
Do we tremble in the day,
When you expose the wicked deeds
We wrought beneath night's pall:
Your light shows off our secret sins
And shames us for them all.

God, in your great anger
All our wasted days are burnt,
Ended like a sorry sigh
For all the pain we've earnt:
Threescore years, threescore and ten –
What is our life to you?
The sum of it but bitterness,
The labour that we do,

Before we pass away –
O, teach us wisdom 'ere we die;
Let us number these our days
Before in dust we lie.
Turn again, O Lord;
How long must we, your servants, wait
For your bright light of morning,
For the darkness to abate?

Let your lovingkindness
Break upon us like the dawn,
Give us gladness to make up
The days we had to mourn,
All the years adversity
Was always at our side;
Prosper now your servants' work,
Your Spirit be our guide!

91

Those who have their refuge
In the dwelling of the Lord,
Who shelter in His shadow,
By His mighty arm assured,
Shall say to Him, 'you are my God,
The tower in which I trust,
My stronghold and my fortress,
Through whose gates no foe can thrust.'

He will slip you free from bondage,
Snap the fowler's snare:
The pestilence that stalks in darkness
Will not reach you there,
Safe beneath His feathers
In the shelter of His wings,
From the flying arrow
And the deadly bite that stings.

With God as shield you will not fear
The wicked weapon's bite,
The sickness that consumes at noon,
Nor terrors of the night –
A thousand fall around you,
And ten thousand at your side,
Yet you will stand untouched alone,
Since you with God abide.

You only need to look and see
The end of evil folk;
With the Lord as refuge
You'll be rescued from their yoke.
No evil dare pursue you,
No plague approach your house:
His angels keep a watch on you,
Misfortune's flames to douse.

They keep you on the righteous road,
And bear you in their hands;
They keep your feet from stumbling
On the stones of foreign lands;
They keep you from the lion's mouth
And from the adder's bite:
You shall walk through scorpions
And scarabs without fright.

God says, 'those who love me
I will lift above the fray:
I will keep from harm all those
Who know my name and pray.
'They will call upon me
In the midst of their despair;
I myself will answer them
And walk beside them there.

'I'll lead them into honour
And deliver them from strife,
Show them my salvation,
Satisfaction and long life.'

92

It is good to thank you, God,
To praise you, O Most High,
To sing to you at daybreak,
And when the night draws nigh;
To tell of all your love
And all your faithfulness each day;
On the harp and lyre,
Joyful melodies to play.

You alone have made me glad,
Have set my heart to soar;
Your mighty works so wonderful
I sing and thank you for.
Your thoughts are firm foundations,
Strong rocks on which we stand:
Yet fools refuse to know you,
Nor your truth to understand.

The wicked think them fruitful
As they sprout and grow like grass,
But they do not see
That in a moment they shall pass.
Evildoers flourish
As a sand house on the shore;
They are washed away
But you endure for evermore.

Your enemies shall perish,
They shall perish at your hand;
The workers of iniquity
Shall scatter and not stand,
But my horn you exalted
As the wild oxen strong;
My eyes shall look in triumph
On all those who did me wrong.

You, Lord, have anointed me
With oil pure and clean;
I shall hear the ruin
Of the cruel and the mean.
Righteous ones shall flourish
As the tree that drinks the Earth
And spread abroad as cedars
In their strength and breadth and girth –
Trees such as are planted
In the garden of the Lord,
To flourish in the courts of God
For ever, their reward.

Even in their old age
They shall bear the sweetest fruit,
Standing strong in vigour
From the leaf tip to the root,
Grounded in the Lord our God,
To show that He is true:
God, you are my rock,
There is no wickedness with you.

93

Glory is the clothing
That adorns our Lord and King!
The Lord put on great garments,
Power is His girdle-ring!
He has built the world so firm
That it cannot be moved;
Everlasting He is God –
His rule from old was proved.

The floods have lifted up their voice,
O God – I call in fright:
The floods rise up with pounding waves
To drown me in their might!
But mightier than many waters,
Than the fiercest sea,
Mightier than towering waves,
Much mightier is He:

The Lord on High, whose testimony,
Love and help is sure!
Holiness surrounds your house,
O God, forever more.

94

Yours, O Lord, is vengeance;
Wrathful recompense is thine –
Yours, O Lord is vengeance;
In your majesty you shine!

Rise up now, O judge of Earth,
Bring down their haughty pride:
How long shall the arrogant
And wicked yet abide?

Look, see how they triumph:
In their evil they delight,
And boast of all their beastly deeds,
Supreme in their own sight.

They pour out words of impudence,
They crush your people down,
They lay your heritage to waste
And spit upon your crown.

They pity not the widow,
They deprive her of her breath,
They set upon the stranger
And the orphans put to death.

They say, 'the Lord won't see it,'
While they murder and enslave,
'How could Jacob's God regard?
What strength has He to save?'

O, most stupid people,
How can you not understand?
Can you be such fools
To not consider His command?

He who crafted every ear,
Can He not hear you?
He who formed each eye,
Shall He not see the things you do?

He corrects the nations –
Why should He not punish now?
The teacher of all peoples,
Did you think He knows not how?

The Lord knows every human thought,
He measures every sigh,
He dwells in every person
And He knows how we will die.

Blessed are the ones
You kindly chasten and correct,
Those whom you instruct, O God,
Whom sin does not infect.

In days of great affliction
You provide them strength and rest,
Until the wicked dig their pits
Which evil deeds infest.

They fall, but God will never fail
His people: He will save,
Nor forsake the sons
Of the inheritance He gave:

Justice to the righteous
Will eventually return,
And the true of heart
To follow justice will not spurn.

Who else would rise and rescue me
When evildoers start?
Who would stand against the wicked?
Who would take my part?

Silenced would have been my soul
If God had passed me by,
But when I cried, 'my foot has slipped!'
He lifted me up high.

A multitude of worries
Were a trouble to my heart,
But God refreshed my soul,
His peace and comfort to impart.

He does no deals with wickedness,
Upon its petty throne
Fashioning its evil laws
With which it snares its own.

In its crooked courts they gather,
Baying righteous blood,
Daring to condemn to death
The innocent and good.

But the Lord is my defence,
The rock on which I rest,
The tower that I trust in;
This charade He does detest!

He will turn their tables:
In the malice that they wrought
He will put them all to silence,
By their evil caught.

95

Come, and let us sing unto the Lord
Our song of praise –
Hearty thanks, rejoicing,
To our rock of rescue raise:

Let us come before Him
With thanksgiving, singing psalms,
Glad before our God so great
Who holds us in His arms.

He is High above all gods,
He holds the depths of Earth,
He commands the mountain heights,
He brought the sea to birth,

His hands prepared the dry land
And He moulded it like clay –
Come and fall in worship,
To our God kneel down and pray,

For He is our maker,
He owns sky and sea and land,
And we are His pasture's people,
Sheep of His own hand.

O that you would hearken
To our father's voice today –
Not like when in Meribah
Your forebears went astray,

At Massah in the wilderness,
When they with hardened hearts
Demanded of and tested Him,
Though they had seen His arts:

'Your forebears put me to the proof,
Detestable were they –
I said, "this wayward generation
Will not know my way,

"They stray within their very soul,
My power they would test,"
And so I swore that they
Should never come into my rest.'

96

All the Earth, sing to the Lord:
A new song sing, with one accord!
O bless the Lord and sing His praise,
His salvation, all your days!
Let His glory be proclaimed
Among the nations, great His name,
And His mighty wonders too:
All the peoples, praise anew!

Great is God, great praise His due;
He only 'midst the gods is true:
Fear Him, for He built the sky,
Fear them not – they are a lie,
The empty idols of men's hands –
Such are gods of foreign lands.

But God, in honoured majesty
And splendour rules His sanctuary.
All you peoples, praise His power,
His strength surpassing every tower;
Ascribe Him honour, bring Him gifts,
Come into His courts to lift
In worship all your trembling praise
As you upon His beauty gaze!

He is Holy; Earth will shake
When the news of His rule breaks
Across the nations He will judge
With equity that none will grudge.

Let the heavens now rejoice!
Let the sea lift up her voice!
Let the trees and fields be glad;
Never Earth such joy has had:
He comes, He comes, to put to proof
And judge the peoples with His truth.

97

The Lord is King: let Earth rejoice,
    The multitudes make glad:
    All the islands of the ocean
        Lift their happy song.
        In encircling cloud
And holy darkness is He clad;
    Righteousness and justice
    Are the rocks He rests upon.

    Fire goes before Him,
    And will eat up all His foes;
When His lightnings lit the world
        The planet shook to see –
        Mountains melt like wax
Before His presence where He goes;
    The heavens saw His splendour
        And declared it by decree!

    All the peoples saw His glory,
        Lord of all the Earth;
    Let the ones who worshipped
        Wicked images be shocked:
    Those who did delight in idols
        That are nothing worth,
    Bow down now before Him,
All false gods before Him knocked!

Zion heard with gladness,
Judah's daughters all took heart,
Because of the good judgements
Of the Lord who rules on high;
Far above these false and senseless gods,
O God, thou art;
Your love is poured out on those
Who wickedness decry.

You preserve your faithful people
From the evil snare;
Light bursts forth in brightness
For the righteous and the true;
Joy erupts upon them,
As on your great love they stare,
And give their thanks to your great name
For all that flows from you!

98

Sing the Lord a new song
For the great things He has done:
His right hand and holy arm
His victory have won.

He has shown salvation,
His deliverance displayed –
In the sight of all the nations
Is His truth arrayed!

He remembered mercy,
He in faithfulness stood fast
To pour it out towards
The house of Israel at last,

And all the Earth from east to west
Has God's salvation seen,
Singing now His praises
To our Lord and God supreme!

Make music with the lyre and harp,
The trumpet and the horn,
And with the voice of melody
May joyful clothes be worn!

Let the sea with thunder roll,
And all its innards shout;
Let the rivers clap with glee,
The mighty hills ring out;

All the world and all who dwell within it
Burst with mirth,
For lo, the Lord, He comes behind them,
Comes to judge the Earth.

With righteousness He judges peoples,
Equity He keeps,
And now He comes to judge the world
And joyful praises reaps!

99

Before the Lord, enthroned as King,
Let the peoples quake;
High above the cherubim,
Let Earth beneath Him shake.
Our Lord sits above them all:
The peoples sing His praise;
Great is He in Zion
And in awe the nations gaze.

Holy is the Lord our God:
His name is set apart;
He established equity
And justice is His art.
He justice brought to Jacob's children,
Righteousness He gave;
Through servants such as Samuel
He Israel did save.

Moses called upon Him,
As did Aaron, as His priest;
From the cloudy pillar
Spoke The Greatest to the least,
And gave to them the Testament,
The law that they should keep –
You answered them, O Lord our God,
And led your straying sheep.

Your forgave their trespasses
And pardoned their offence,
When, upon your holy hill,
You dealt out recompense.
Exalt the Lord our God:
Bow down and stoop beneath His feet!
Worship Him, the holy One
Upon His mighty seat.

100

All the Earth, be jubilant –
In joyfulness sing praise!
Come with gladness to the Lord
And serve Him all your days.

In the Lord take greatest pleasure,
Know that He is God:
It is He that made us,
We are guided by His rod,

The people of His pasture –
We are His beloved sheep –
So enter in His gates with thanks,
His courts with praises heap,

And bless the name of Him who gave you life,
With steadfast love:
His grace and faith for ever last,
For all His saints above.

101

To you, O Lord, I sing
A song of faithfulness and truth:
Let me walk in wisdom,
Let perfection be my proof.

When, Lord, will you come to me
And show the righteous way?
I will walk with purity of heart
Until that day.

Keeping in the confines
Of your house of holy grace,
I refuse to look upon
A counsel of disgrace;

I reject unfaithfulness,
And evil won't abide –
These things shall not cling to me
Nor in my true heart hide.

To crooked ways I will not lean,
Nor wicked folk befriend –
Those who slander neighbours
And their secret gossip send,

I will put to silence,
Nor endure a haughty eye;
An arrogance of heart
I will not countenance to lie.

I will fix my gaze
Upon the faithful of the Earth:
They will dwell with me,
And be my servants of great worth,

Those who walk in purity,
In honesty complete;
None within my walls will dwell
Who practice cruel deceit.

One who whispers falsehood
Will not linger in my sight:
Day by day I silence those
Who stray from what is right,

And cast out from the city,
That fair dwelling of the Lord,
All who lust for evil –
This will be their just reward.

102

Please, O Lord, please hear my prayer,
My crying and my tears –
Let them rise before you,
And incline your listening ears.

Do not hide your face away,
Nor leave me in distress:
In the day I cry to you,
Please answer my address!

All my days consume away,
Like smoke they disappear:
All my bones are burnt up
In the furnace of my fear;

My heart hangs as a heavy weight,
It wilts as withered grass;
I forget to eat or drink
As dreadful hours pass.

My face is sore with groaning,
My bones jut out from my skin;
I am like a ragged owl,
A vulture wearing thin

And haunting empty ruins,
Where no crumb of joy is found,
Watching like a lonely sparrow
To his housetop bound.

I dare not go abroad to hear
   Mine enemies pour scorn,
   In their rage reviling me –
A cruel pact have they sworn,

And all I have is ashes left
   To be my daily bread:
My drink is soured by bitter tears,
   Weeping from my bed.

I am made a misery
   Because of your disdain;
In your wrath you took me up
   And cast me down again.

All my hours are fading
   Like a shadow in the Sun,
And my body wastes away
Like grass when summer's done.

You endure for ever, Lord,
   As generations wane:
You will surely show your pity
   To your land again.

Zion sits and waits for you,
   Your mercy's time has come;
Your servants love her every stone
   And for her sake are glum.

Let the nations fear your name,
The kings of Earth your might:
May your glory shine from Zion
    In their constant sight.

You have heard the poor cry out
And not despised their plea;
You have turned, that all their humble prayer
    Might answered be.

All those who come after,
They shall hear and praise the Lord,
When we write your gracious deeds,
    And of your mighty sword,

And how you look with favour
From your high place set apart,
Above the Earth, but looking down,
    Salvation to impart.

You hear the sighs and agony
Of those who, fearful, lie;
All who sit imprisoned and ashamed,
    Condemned to die:

You will come and visit them,
And set the captives free,
That throughout Jerusalem
Your wondrous praise may be!

The peoples then will gather
From the nations spread abroad,
Those from every kingdom
Come as one to praise the Lord!

You it was who sapped my strength,
Who set me on hard ways;
I cry to you, O God,
Do not cut short my feeble days.

Your years will endure –
Eternal, you laid out the Earth;
You hold high the heavens
That by you were brought to birth;

Still, these things will perish,
As old rags to be cast off,
But you will never fail,
Nor fall a prey to rust nor moth.

These too will continue:
All of those who do what's right,
And your servants' children
Live for ever in your sight.

103

Bless the Lord, my heart and soul,
And all that is within me!
Bless the Lord, my heart and soul,
Never to forget
All His happy benefits
His gracious love did win me,
Who heals my frail body
And my sins to right has set;

Who drew me from the pit
Wherein my life was sure to fall,
Who set a crown of love and favour
On my worthless head;
Who sees His children's hunger
And in mercy feeds them all;
Who renewed my ageing frame
And gave me youth instead!

The Lord insists on righteousness,
And He will have it done:
He as judge gives recompense
For all who are oppressed.
By Moses He was known –
By Him was Israel's freedom won,
And to our generations shown
That God's great works are best.

Mercy and compassion
Fill His essence to the brim:
Slowly does His anger smoulder,
But His kindness quick;
Not for ever angry
Accusations stand with Him,
For He will burn our sins away
Though they be dense and thick.

He will not reward us
For our wickedness in kind;
His mercy reaches further
Than the heavens stretch above.
So far as is the East from West,
Our sins He flings from mind,
When He, as father to a child,
Shows His forgiving love.

Those who fear the Lord
Will never loving mercy lack,
For God will not forget
How He has formed us from the dust:
Our days depart as withered grass
That in the sun dies back;
We flourish as a feeble flower
From the field thrust.

When the wind goes over it,
So suddenly it's gone:
It's place shall not remember
What so shortly there took root,

But we will be remembered
By the everlasting One
For He shows such goodness
To all those who bear good fruit,

Who keep to His commandments
And His covenant obey –
To their children's children
He will righteousness bestow.
He has built His kingdom
In high heaven this great day,
And will have dominion
Over all who dwell below.

Bless the Lord, you angels –
All who carry out His will;
Bless the Lord, you hosts in light
Who hearken to His word;
Bless the Lord, you wondrous works
He did with Spirit fill,
In every place – my heart and soul,
Now sing and bless the Lord!

104

My soul will sing and bless the Lord –
My God, how great you are!
The garment of my God is light,
More bright than any star:

Honour is His clothing,
And great majesty His cloak –
The heavens like a canvas were
Unfolded as He spoke.

Your house, God, you founded
On the waters of the sky;
The clouds you ride as chariots,
On wings of wind you fly –

The whirlwind speaks your messages,
The fiery blaze is yours,
To carry out your will within
A world that heeds your laws.

You drilled the Earth's foundations deep,
That it should never stray,
And wrapped the ocean's mantle round it
In the ancient day,

Then shrunk the seas to their right place,
Uncovering the land,
Where the river valleys lie
And hills rise up to stand.

Earth and sea, they fear you,
And obey your thundering voice;
The boundaries of the waters
Were appointed at your choice

That they should not return again
To swallow up the Earth,
Except the brooks and streams you set
To flow down to the surf.

These you made for drinking,
For the wild ass and the beast,
And birds in branches, building nests
Whom you love not the least –

You water from the heavens
And the Earth brings forth her fruit;
The singing birds, they please you,
And the tender-springing shoot.

The grass grows up for cattle,
And sweet plants meet all our needs –
They are the food you give, on which
Your whole creation feeds,

With wine to gladden weary hearts
And Oil to make us shine,
Bread to fill our bellies
That our hearts be strong and fine.

The trees God plants are full of sap,
His cedars tall and strong,
That the birds may nest in joy
And fill the air with song.

His mountains are the home of goats;
In cliffs the rabbits thrive,
The lions seek their prey of God
That they may stay alive.

You made the Moon to mark the months,
The Sun the night and day,
Setting him to wax and wane
And seasons to portray.

He hides His face and darkness falls,
The forest creatures creep,
Then He rises up and they
Return to lie and sleep

In the dens you built for them –
The beasts of day and night,
Each with their own habitation,
Precious in your sight.

In the morning, people rise
And go about their work;
They labour until evening falls,
When back to bed they walk.

O God, all this is yours –
All this, your mighty work of art!
In your wisdom you designed
The world to please your heart.

You filled it with your creatures,
They which dwell on land and sea –
There move many, small and great,
Beneath the ships we see:

There the deep leviathan,
That plays among the depths –
Even he must look to you for food
With which he's kept.

You provide, they gather:
With an open hand you give
To all your creatures all they need
That they might eat, and live.

If you hide your face away,
Then pain and trouble lurk;
When you take away their breath
They turn to dust and murk,

But you send your spirit back
To endlessly create;
You renew the Earth's green face,
And you restore its fate.

God, your glory will endure
For ever – we rejoice
At your works of splendour,
All obeying your great voice.

Look upon the land and it
Will tremble at your gaze;
Only touch the mountains
And a fearsome smoke they raise!

I will sing to you, my God,
For all my Earthly time –
I will give you daily praise
Of music, dance and rhyme.

So I pray, my song shall please you –
Bless the Lord, my soul!
For He destroys all evil,
But with goodness will console.

105

Give thanks to God, and call on Him:
So let His strength be shown;
Let His deeds among the peoples
Of all lands be known.

Sing to Him your praises,
Sing the miracle He's done;
Praise His Holy name with joy
And let His fame be sung.

Let your hands be lifted high,
All you who seek the Lord,
Seek His strength, and by
His mighty countenance be awed:

Remember all the gracious deeds
His mighty arm has won,
Ponder all the wonders
And the judgements He has done.

Abraham His servant's seed,
O Jacob's chosen child,
Know that He, the Lord, is God:
His name be not defiled,

For His righteous judgement
Stretches over all the Earth,
He holds fast the covenant
With us, as of great worth.

He is ever mindful
Of the promise that He made,
Which across a thousand
Generations would not fade:

The oath He swore to Abraham,
His pact with Isaac sealed,
The statute He set up for Jacob,
Not to be repealed –

Forever, everlasting,
Would His covenant endure:
'Yours will be the land of Canaan
Now and evermore.

'This is thine inheritance,'
He told their little band,
Though they were but few
And mere sojourners in the land.

From nation unto nation
They went wondering far and wide,
In kingdoms and with other diverse
Peoples to abide.

He suffered none to harm them,
Even kings He would chastise:
'Do not hurt my peoples,
Mine anointed don't despise.'

Then He brought a famine on the land,
They had no bread:
Yet He had sent Joseph,
That through him they might be fed.

He was sold to slavery,
In Egypt he was bound,
His feet were locked in fetters
And his neck was ringed around,

But he heard the Word of God –
The future he could see,
So the king released him:
He from bondage was set free,

Appointed as the lord to rule
The royal house instead,
And all the king's possessions
Must be ordered as he said.

His will prevailed over princes,
Wise men he'd instruct,
And his family, Israel's own,
To Egypt he'd induct.

So it was that Jacob
Came to dwell upon Ham's land,
And His chosen people there
Did prosper at God's hand.

They became too numerous
According to their foes,
Whose hearts had turned to hatred,
Who afflicted them with woes,

Who dealt in crafty subtlety
To put this people down,
Till God picked Moses
And his brother Aaron for renown.

He chose these as His servants
To speak of the signs He'd show,
The wonders sent because
They would not let His people go:

So upon the land of Ham
He sent three days of dark,
But they wouldn't listen;
To His words they would not hark.

Then He turned the waters
Of their river into blood;
All their fish were poisoned,
Yet they had not understood,

So He sent a force of frogs
To cover all the land,
Even from the poorest hut
To royal chambers grand;

He brought on them thick clouds of flies
And swarms of biting gnats,
He sent them hail instead of rain
And knocked their harvest flat;

He brought down flames of lightning,
And their vines and trees were dead;
He brought up teams of grasshoppers
And swarms of locusts bred –

These devoured every plant
Still standing in the field,
But yet they would not hearken
To the signs He had revealed.

So He smote their firstborn sons,
Through all of Egypt – gone,
The first fruits of their strength,
He slew them every single one.

Then they sent His people out
With silver and with gold;
None of these His children stumbled,
Neither young nor old:

Egypt at the last
Was very glad to see them leave,
Filled with dread for all the sorrows
That she had to grieve.

He sent a cloud to cover them by day,
And through the night,
He sent a burning fire
That would be their guiding light.

They asked for food, He satisfied them,
Sending heaven's bread;
He cleft the rock that water
Filled the dried-up river bed.

He remembered what He'd said
To Abraham, His own;
He brought out His people, singing
In a joyful tone;

He gave them many nations' lands,
The promised holy soil,
So they took possession
Of the fruits of others' toil.

He did this that they might hold fast
The statutes of His word,
And faithfully obey
All the commandments they had heard.

106

Alleluia! Praise the Lord
For all His graciousness!
His wondrous works are more
Than any person can express –

His praise beyond all telling;
Meagre words cannot suffice
To frame His endless faithfulness,
His love without a price.

Blessed are all those
Who always do what's just and right;
Keep me, God, amongst the people
Favoured in your sight.

When the day when you will save us
Finally arrives,
Visit me and let me see
The joy your help revives.

I shall see prosperity
Your chosen ones enjoy;
I shall join with them in gladness
Nothing can destroy.

O God! Show us your mercy:
Like our forebears steeped in sin,
We have wrought in wickedness,
In wrong we did begin.

They regarded little
Your great wonders done of old,
When with overflowing love
You shattered Egypt's hold:

Already when you brought them
Through the Red Sea, they rebelled,
Yet to make your power known
Your anger you withheld;

For your name's sake you saved them,
You drove away the sea,
You led them through depths
As through the desert, set them free,

And saved them from adversaries –
You slipped them from their hand,
And brought them through from trouble
To a safe and pleasant land.

As for those, their enemies,
The sea swallowed them all –
Many rushed in cruel pursuit,
And every one did fall.

Then your people sang your praise,
For they believed your word,
Yet soon enough they did forget,
And discontent was heard.

They wouldn't wait for guidance,
By cravings they were caught;
To test the love and strength of God
They in the desert sought.

He gave them what they wanted,
But sent sapping sickness too,
Then against their leaders
Wicked jealousy they knew:

Of Aaron and of Moses,
Who had guided them so well;
Dathan and the company
Of Abiram thus fell.

No sooner was their challenge made,
The Earth opened beneath
And swallowed up the lot of them
Who had devised such grief.

A fire, too, you kindled
And the wicked you destroyed,
Who forged a golden calf
And in its worship were employed:

They cast off the glory
Poured upon them by their God,
To serve instead the image
Of an ox that bears the rod.

They forgot the God who saved them
For a lump of clay;
The God who did such deeds of might
For one that feeds on hay.

He had worked such wonders
In the fearsome land of Ham,
He had wrought such terror
When the sea burst as a dam!

He would now destroy them
For their heartless treachery,
Had not Moses stood
And for his people made his plea.

So God did not consume them,
And He turned away His wrath,
Though they mocked the Promised Land
And would not tread His path.

In their tents they murmured,
For in Him they had no faith;
To Him they would not listen
When He sought to bring them safe:

He swore to overthrow them then
And lifted up His hand
To scatter their descendents
Amidst every distant land.

They were led astray
To many nations, far and near:
They placed their vain allegiance
In the no-god Baal of Peor;

They even filled their stomachs
With things offered to the dead,
Spurning God's great love,
Provoking angry plague instead.

Their evil deeds had swallowed them:
To evil they had strayed,
But Phineas begged God for mercy,
And the plague was stayed.

He was counted righteous
By their sons through every age,
Yet still again at Meribah
They stirred up God's great rage.

There even faithful Moses
Had to suffer for their sake,
For in bitter spirit
He spoke rash words by mistake.

They did not destroy the other nations –
God's command –
But mingled with the peoples
That inhabited their land,

Following in wicked ways,
Which were a vicious snare,
Worshipping the lifeless idols
They encountered there.

Their own sons and daughters,
Which God gave them as a gift,
They slew on crooked altars
As a sacrifice to lift –

Evil spirits they pursued,
And shed their infants' blood;
Their own sons and daughters
In their guiltless childhood.

So they did defile the land,
Polluting all the ground,
Soaked in blood while praise
To Canaan's idols did resound –

Their wicked deeds betrayed them,
With all false gods did they whore,
And stirred the wrath of God
Against the ones He chose before.

He couldn't stand the sight of them,
Whose deeds He did detest,
And gave them up to other nations,
As their slaves oppressed.

They were ruled over
Not by God, who loved them so,
But by cruel tyrants
Who could only hate bestow.

Thus in their subjection
They endured their rivals' yoke;
Each time God delivered them,
His covenant they broke.

Through their own abominations
They were brought so low,
Yet God saw their trouble
And their mournful sigh did know.

He recalled the covenant
That they so oft forgot;
In His faithful mercy,
He'd not leave them there to rot:

He made them to know pity
At their adversaries' hand,
He gave them hope they might come back
And know the Promised Land.

Save us, God, and gather us
From where we have been thrown;
We will thank and praise your name –
Remember us, your own!

Blessed be the Lord,
The God of Israel, evermore –
Alleluia and Amen,
Let all the people roar!

107

The Lord's love lasts for ever:
For His graciousness give thanks,
All you from your foes redeemed:
The rescued in your ranks,
Gathered from the eastern hills,
From North and South and West –
Among you those who went astray
And found no place of rest.

They lingered in the desert wastes
In hunger and in thirst,
Their famished spirits fainting,
As they feared the very worst;
They cried unto the Lord for help,
Who heard them in distress,
Who brought their feet back to the way
And carried them, no less,

Until they reached the city where
Their souls in safety dwell:
Let them thank the Lord
And of His gracious wonders tell!
He satisfies the hungry heart,
The longing soul, with good.
O give Him praise, all you
Who through His rescue understood!

Others sat in darkness,
Shrouded in death's shadows deep;
Locked in chains of misery,
In fetters doomed to weep.
They suffered there because they spoke
Against the Word of God,
They cast away His counsels
And in crooked ways they trod.

So they reaped but bitterness,
And heaviness of heart,
When they stumbled on the road
They'd none to share their part.
Yet they cried to God
From in that dungeon of despair;
He came to their deliverance,
He sat beside them there,

He chased away death's shadows
And the darkness He dispelled,
The iron bonds so strong He smashed,
The iron bars He felled,
He broke the doors of bronze asunder:
His great goodness praise!
Others took to paths of fools
And to unrighteous ways.

They suffered plagues in all they did,
Because they worked such wrong;
Their soul could not be satisfied,
To death they might have gone,

But they called to God,
Who brought them out of their distress;
With His Word He healed them
And now let them confess
Their thanks to God for all His goodness
On His children wrought:
Let them tell with shouts of joy,
Who by His acts were bought!

Some set sail upon the sea,
The oceans wide and steep;
They have seen the works of God
And wonders of the deep:
At His Word the wind grew strong
And lifted high the waves,
Tossed them to the heavens' height
Then down to secret caves.

Grievous was their peril
And their spirit waned away;
Reeling like a drunkard,
At their wits' end did they pray
And begged for help in trouble,
so God heard their sore distress,
And made the sea be still
So that the wind and waves were less.

He brought them to a haven,
And at rest He set their ship –
Let them thank the Lord
Who helps His children when they slip.
In the congregation of the people,
Sing His praise!
In the council of the elders
Honour Him always!

He stops the springs and rivers,
Turns lush lands to empty thirst,
Makes deserts of the fruitful fields,
By salty water curst,
Wherever dwell the wicked,
To rebuke them for their sin;
But gives the poor and hungry
Homes of plenty to dwell in.

For them the parchèd wilderness
Becomes a soothing pool,
The thirsty ground springs water
And feeds vineyards by His rule:
They sow their fields,
By a fruitful harvest satisfied;
He blesses them, that they
And all their herds are multiplied.

He pours contempt on princes,
Lets them wander trackless wastes,
Those who would exalt themselves,
Diminished and debased,

Marred by grave misfortune
And by sorrow carried down,
Whilst those they held in misery
Are raised to high renown.

As flocks of sheep their families
Will grow, and now rejoice,
Whilst those who walked in wickedness
Will see and lose their voice.
Whoever would have wisdom,
Let him ponder all these things,
And see how loving is the Lord
And what good deeds He brings!

108

O God, my heart is ready:
I will sing and give you praise –
God, my heart is ready
This glad anthem now to raise!

O awake, my soul, and sing
As on the harp and lyre:
Play your music loud and bright,
The daybreak to inspire!

Your dawn, O Lord, is rising:
I will give my thanks to you;
In amongst the peoples
I will boldly praise you too,

For your love and kindness
Is far higher than the sky:
Your faithfulness extends
Beyond the clouds, as heaven high!

God, be now exalted
Far beyond the starry dome –
May your glory gleam
All round the Earth that is our home.

Rescue your beloved ones –
Give answer to my plea,
And by your hand of righteousness
Reach down and set us free.

God spoke by His holy word,
    Which cannot be denied:
'I will triumph over Shechem,
    Succoth I'll divide,

'Gilead and Ephraim
    And Manasseh are mine;
Judah is the sceptre used
    To do my will divine.

'Moab is my wash-pot
    I will rinse out in my wrath;
At Edom I shall cast my shoe,
    And trammel there a path;

'Over all Philistia
    My shouts of triumph ring';
Who now to the city strong,
    To Edom's gates, will bring?

Haven't you forgotten us,
    O God, or put us by?
Will you not go out again
    To lead the battle cry,

Strengthening our armies,
Bringing help against our foe?
    All Earthly help is vain
Unless with your support we go.

Through God we will do mighty acts,
Perform such wondrous deeds,
For God, He is the One
Who will tread down our enemies.

109

End your empty silence –
Answer me, God of my praise;
Hear the mouth of malice
And the wicked things it says.

In treachery they speak against me,
Lies are on their lips:
All around, their hateful words
Are poised like sharpened tips.

They fought me for no reason,
Cursing me without a cause,
Returning for the love I gave them
Only gaping jaws.

You know how I prayed for them,
Upon my bended knee,
But evil is their payment
For the good they got from me.

I showered them with goodness,
And yet how do they repay?
A pot of seething hatred –
'Appoint over him,' they say,

'A wicked man to govern him,
And put at his right hand
Someone to accuse him
And condemn him at the stand.

'When it comes to judgement,
Let great guilt in him be found.
Let it be accounted sin,
His prayer's pathetic sound.

'Let his life be short in span –
Make sure his days are few,
And give to someone else his goods
And his position too.

'Let his wife be widowed,
Let his children beg for bread,
Let them all as orphans weep
Because their dad is dead –

'So what if they must wander
Far and wide to look for food,
Or subsist on desert dust
In their decrepitude?

'Let a wealthy creditor
Seize hold of all he's got,
Let greedy strangers fall
Upon his house and take the lot!

'Let it all be plundered,
What he worked so hard to gain;
Let no-one who has any faith
Or love for him remain.

'Do not have compassion
On the children that he leaves –
Let his line be ended,
Give his portion up to thieves!

'Let his name be blotted out,
Let all his seed die off,
And let his father's every evil deed
Be held aloft.

'Let no sinful murmur
Of his mother be forgot,
Store up all their misdeeds
And do not erase a jot!

'Let God remember their mistakes,
Obliterate their name,
And root out this family,
Discarded in their shame.'

They are false accusers.
They say, 'he did not keep faith:
The poor he persecuted,
From him nobody was safe.

'He sought to kill the broken-hearted,
Stole from those in need,
And he must be punished
For his negligence and greed.

'His mouth was filled with curses
   And of blessings he gave none;
He clothed himself with curses
   For he loved them as a son.

'Sin seeped into his body
   And like oil slaked his bones –
Let him fall according
   To the curses that he owns,

'The belt he wrapped about him,
   And the sin that was his cloak:
Let him be destroyed
   For all the wickedness he spoke.'

Lord, you know that these are lies –
   My ruin do they seek.
Repay now mine accusers
   For the evil that they speak!

Deal with me, O God,
   According to your mighty name;
Sweet is your great faithfulness –
   Deliver me from shame,

For I have no other help,
   My prospects are so poor;
My heart is melting in me
   For I cannot win this war:

I fade away to nothing
Like a shadow in the night,
Shaken like a locust,
So disgusting in their sight.

I am faint through fasting
And my knees from prayer grow sore;
All my flesh is wasting
And my skin is cracked and raw.

I am a reproach to them:
I humbly kneel for grace,
But seeing me, they shake their heads
And scorn is on their face.

Help me, O my Lord, my God,
For I am all but spent;
Save me in your loving mercy –
I my sins repent!

Let them know that you have done it,
You stretch out your hand
To rescue me from mine accusers,
Show your reprimand!

They're the ones who curse me,
But there's blessing in your voice –
Let them be confounded
While your servants yet rejoice.

Let those false accusers
Be ashamed for what they spoke,
Let them be wrapped up
In their disgrace as in a cloak.

So all who look and see them
Will know I am not at fault,
While I sing out thanks to you,
Set free from mine assault:

In the midst of multitudes
My mouth shall shout your praise;
I will give great thanks to you,
Throughout all my days.

Because beside the needy
And the helpless you stand fast,
To save them from such evil
Condemnation's icy blast!

110

The Lord God said to my Lord,
'Sit thou here at my right hand,
And I will make your enemies
Fall down at your command.'

May the Lord empower you,
Your sceptre holding strong,
To rule the world from Zion
'Midst all those who did you wrong.

Into true nobility
This day you're born anew;
As the dawn brings forth the morn
And girds its face with dew,

So you freshly sparkle
On the holy mountain fair;
For God has sworn and won't revoke
The oath He promised there:

'After that Malchizedek
Your fathers knew of yore,
You will be a priest
In his great order, evermore.'

The king, O God, at your right hand
Shall mighty rulers smite;
They will totter helpless
When his anger comes to bite.

When, as all the nations' judge,
　　He reigns in majesty,
When the heads which haughtiness
　　Had lifted smitten be,

He shall drink from brimming brooks
　　That flow beside the way,
And his head in righteousness
　　Be lifted high that day!

111

Alleluia! To my God
My whole heart sets its thanks
Amongst the congregation,
In the faithful children's ranks:
The works of God are mighty,
They are honourable and great;
They are our souls' supreme delight;
For them we watch and wait.

His righteousness endures eternal;
Through His loving grace
He sent us a memorial
To show our mortal race:
He fed His fearing children,
And He made with them a pact,
He gave them choice inheritance –
With power did He act

And poured upon His people
All their fathers thirsted for;
All His deeds are truthful,
All His just commandments sure.
His words stand fast for ever,
True for every one He's made;
Eternally redemption
He upon His faithful laid,

Commanding that His covenant
With them would never cease.
How awesome is His holy name!
O, let His praise increase!
Wisdom has its well-spring
In the fear of the Lord;
To those who set their hearts on Him
Great knowledge He'll afford.

112

Alleluia!
Those who fear the Lord are ever blest;
Their righteousness endures eternal –
Never will it rest.

Their descendents too will wax
Most mighty in the land,
Because they have delighted
To obey the Lord's command.

This faithful generation
Will enjoy a soul of health,
Their houses will be filled
With heaven's riches, precious wealth.

Darkness cannot conquer them:
For them there shines a light,
Radiant with grace
And with compassion blazing bright.

It goes well with those who lend
With generosity,
Who are just in all their dealings,
In sincerity:

They will not be shaken,
Nor their righteous names forgot;
They will be for ever held
When other men are not.

When the evil tidings come
They will not be afraid:
They trust in the Lord their God,
On Him their heart is stayed.

Their heart remains steadfast,
And for nothing will they fear;
They shall see their fearsome foes
Fade out and disappear.

Their righteous deeds are kept:
They've freely given to the poor;
Their head is exalted
With great honour ever more.

The wicked shall look on at this
And gnash their teeth in woe;
Desires of the wicked
To oblivion will go.

113

Alleluia: praise Him,
All you servants of the Lord!
Praise His name, let praise
And blessing ever be outpoured.

From the Sun's first rising
To the setting of the same,
Pour out praise before the Lord,
For blessed is His name.

He is high above the heavens,
Over all the Earth,
Over every nation,
Over land and sky and surf:

There is none like God
That has His throne set up so high,
Far beyond the farthest stars,
Beyond the depths of sky,

Yet puts on humility
To look upon our land,
To come and bring the needy comfort,
Take them by the hand,

Lift them from the ashes,
From the dust lift up the poor,
And their rightful place
Amongst all blessed men restore.

He sets them with the princes
Of His people, loved the same
As all who humbly serve Him
And sing praises to His name.

He helps the barren woman,
Brings her back into the house
To be the joyful mother
Of the children of her spouse.

114

When Israel came from Egypt,
And when Jacob thence broke free,
We left a land whose language
Was to us a mystery.

We founded Israel, our dominion,
Judah was our home:
The sea, it saw us coming
And drew back its wave and foam.

Jordan fled before us,
And the mountains ran away;
The hills skipped off like frightened sheep
That we might cross that day.

What worried you, O sea, O Jordan,
That you fled in haste?
What moved you, hills and mountains,
That as goaded rams you raced?

The presence of the Lord –
The Earth will tremble in His wake!
The presence of the Lord –
The land and sea and sky will shake!

He turns the hard and dried up rock
Into a pool so sweet;
The flint becomes a well of water
Springing at our feet!

115

To your great name, O God, give we
All glory for our gain,
Not to our own feeble strength,
Since your grace holds the reign.
Why should all the nations mock us,
'Where is now their God?'
Our God abides in heaven,
But He guides us with His rod.

He does whatever pleases Him:
To these He pays no heed,
Who craft of gold and silver
Empty idols in their greed.
Mouths they mould, which cannot speak,
And eyes that cannot see;
They fashion ears that cannot hear,
And feet that lifeless be.

Their noses know no scent,
Their icy hands no form can feel,
And yet these worthless works they worship
As if they were real!
Not a whisper do they make;
In silence will they rust,
As will all who make them and
In loveless trinkets trust.

But you, O Israel, trust the Lord:
He is your help and shield;
House of Aaron, trust the Lord,
Whose mercy is revealed;
You that know and fear Him,
Let no terror take your nerve –
He alone has might and strength,
His shield will not swerve.

The Lord, He has remembered us;
Sweet blessings will He give
On all who love and fear Him,
All Israel while we live.
Small and great, He loves them all,
Their children shall increase,
And His loving blessings, if they serve Him,
Shall not cease.

He it is who made the heavens,
Where He sits enthroned;
He it is who made the Earth,
Which to us all He loaned.
The dead, they do not praise Him,
For in silence do they lie,
But we forever will raise praises
Far beyond the sky!

116

I love the Lord.
He heard me, and my voice to Him was dear;
On the day I cried to Him,
To me He bent His ear.

I was held on every side,
Trapped by the snares of death;
The agonies of Hell itself
Oppressed my every breath.

In my depths of sorrow,
In the torment of my grief,
I called out to the Lord
And begged my master for relief.

God is good and gracious,
His compassion without bound;
From Him my soul, pressed very low,
Deliverance has found!

He looks upon the simple,
And He saves them when distressed:
Turn again, my weary soul,
Brought safely to your rest.

God to me was gracious,
Saved my spirit from death's pall;
Mine eyes He dried of tears
And my feet He let not fall –

So I walk before Him,
Even in the land of life,
Though I thought to perish
For so bitter was my strife.

I had said in mine alarm
That everyone spoke lies –
But how shall I repay the Lord
Now that from death I rise?

No falsehood are His benefits:
Salvation is His gift,
And so the precious cup
Of His remembrance I shall lift.

I will call upon God's name,
I will fulfil my vows,
In front of all the people
His great praise shall I arouse.

I will risk my very life
In speaking what is right:
The death of faithful servants
Is most precious in His sight.

Lord, I am your humble servant,
By your handmaid born,
From bondage you have freed me
And my fetters you have torn,

Adopting me as your own son –
And so I praise your name,
Offering my sacrifice
Of thanks up to the same.

In the presence of your people
I will keep my word,
In Jerusalem and in
The House of my great Lord!

117

All you nations, Praise the Lord!
All you peoples, make accord,
For great is His most steadfast love –
His favour fixed for you above
Where He reigns, eternal King:
Alleluia, let us sing!

118

Give thanks to the Lord for He is good:
O praise His name for ever!
All priests and people, now proclaim
His mercy sure together!

All who fear the Lord, give shout;
I know His love for me –
When I called He answered,
And He set my spirit free!

The Lord is at my side – take heed,
For what now shall I fear?
Who shall make me tremble,
When He surely shall appear?

And save me from the tumult,
My sweet refuge from my foes;
The Lord is with the one who loves Him
Wheresoe'er he goes.

Trust the Lord: there is no point
In trusting things of flesh,
In the pride of princes
Or the strength of iron mesh;

No confidence is found in them
Which seem to wax but wain,
Which tomorrow lose the strength
And fame today they gain.

All the nations of the Earth
encompassed to attack;
Trusting in the name of God
I drove their armies back.

They hemmed me in on every side,
And I was caught and trapped;
On God's name and strength I called,
And I drove them back.

Bees, they buzzed about me,
Like a fire in thorns to crack,
But by God's great name and strength to save
I drove them back.

I was pressed by deadly force,
Was driven to the brink,
But God's hand, it held me up,
So that I did not sink.

He pushed me back upon them,
Drove my fickle foes away;
My God and salvation,
My great strength from day to day!

Joyful shouts ascend to Him
From where the righteous dwell,
His right hand does mighty deeds
And makes all things be well.

His right hand has raised us up,
His arm does mighty acts:
I shall not die, but live,
And shall declare these wondrous facts!

The Lord has struck me sorely,
He has punished me for sins,
But not given me to death;
In Him my life begins.

Open now before me,
I command you, righteous gates,
And I shall enter in
Where every righteous one prostrates:

The gate of God, through which we pass
To sing to Him our thanks;
You have answered me
And I shall praise you from the ranks!

The stone that all the builders
Counted naught and threw away
Is become the stone on which
Your Temple stands today –

So wonderful a doing
Our good Lord's must surely be
And is marvellous to all
Whose eyes look on and see.

This day is a blessed day,
The day the Lord has made:
Let our hearts rejoice and soar,
Let gladness now cascade!

Come, O Lord, and save us now,
We humbly pray to thee:
Come, O Lord, and send us now
Our new prosperity.

Blessed is the One who comes
In God's name here to tread;
We bless you from His holy house,
The children He has fed.

The Lord, He is our light,
He guides us on our pilgrim way
And links us to His altar
By the cords of love today.

You are God, and all my thanks
And praise I give to you:
O give Him thanks, for God is good,
His mercy ever new!

119

~1: Aleph~

Blessed are the feet
That do not wander from the way;
Blessed are the hearts
Which from the Lord's law do not stray.

Blessed are the minds which from
His judgement never part,
The souls that seek the Lord with all
Their body, mind and heart –

Those who work no wickedness,
Who trust His guiding hand:
You, O Lord, instruct us
That we keep to your command.

O, that I had strength to stay
The straight and righteous road!
O, that I might every moment
Live within your code!

Then I should not need to fear
Nor ever be ashamed:
One who has regard
For your command cannot be blamed.

When I learn your judgements
I will pour out hearty thanks,
When with undiminished joy
I join the righteous ranks –

I will learn to keep your laws,
Your statutes guide my thought;
O God, do not forsake the one
Who after you has sought!

~2: Beth~

How shall they of tender years,
Midst all the vice of youth,
Cleanse their path of lure and lust
And linger in the truth?

I sought you with my whole heart,
How I longed to keep your word –
Do not let me slip astray
From what from you I heard!

Your voice spoke deep within me,
In my heart I kept it hid,
To meditate upon your Word
And of my sin be rid.

Blessed are you, Lord and God –
O teach me your decrees,
And with my lips I will proclaim
Your judgements as you please.

Your words are greater treasure
    Than the riches of the Earth;
Pure delight, before which
    Other things are nothing worth.

I meditate on your commands,
    I contemplate your deeds;
I set my thought upon your way
    And follow where it leads.

I have the greatest pleasure
    To obey as you command,
And I will not forget the orders
    Issued at your hand.

~3: Gimel~

Lord, I am your servant:
    Do me good, that I might live;
To your Word, my only gift,
    My loyalty, I give.

Open up mine eyes, O Lord,
    That I might see for sure
The wonders of creation,
And throughout it all your law.

I am but a stranger
In the fruitful Earth you made;
    Let me see and know
The way of goodness that you laid.

My very soul is eaten up
With longing, night and day,
To see your righteous judgements
And the recompense you pay:

You put down the arrogant,
The wayward soul is curst;
Take from me rebuke and shame,
Since after you I thirst!

I hearkened to your testimony,
Though the pain was raw –
For rulers sat and spat at me,
Because I kept your law.

I meditate upon your statutes:
These are my delight;
I trust your faithful counsel
When it comes to wrong and right.

~4: *Daleth*~

My soul is sleeping in the dust,
By sorrow I am pressed:
I long for you to give me life
And let my spirit rest!

I admit my faults to you,
The erring of my ways;
Lord, you answer me I know:
Please teach the one who prays.

Make me yet to comprehend
The way of your command,
Let me meditate upon
The works wrought by your hand!

My soul will melt away,
Dissolved in tears of my grief:
O raise me from this bitter place
And make my biding brief.

Snatch me off the way of falsehood,
From that deathly door;
Set me by your grace
Upon the road you trod before:

I have chosen truth to follow,
I beheld your step,
I hold fast your judgement
And your testament I've kept –

Let me not be put to shame,
Your Word has set me free
To run the way of righteousness,
My heart at liberty!

~5: He~

Teach me, Lord, the way
That I must walk: I will be true
And keep upon the righteous path
That I receive from you.

Until the ending of my days,
With my entire heart,
I will keep the law
Of understanding you impart:

Lead me, Lord –
I cannot see without you, be my light;
Guide me by your testimonies,
Which are my delight;

Incline my heart to follow you,
And unjust gain reject;
Turn my gaze from vanities
That would my soul infect!

Lord, I beg you, let me start
Upon the way of life,
Confirming what you promised
To your servant in my strife,

And to all who fear you,
Who look for your release,
And let the dread reproaches
Of the wicked turn and cease!

Your judgements, Lord, are good and true –
I long for your command,
And trust that, in your righteousness,
In life I yet will stand.

~6: Waw~

Let your love shine into my life
Like sunlight into glass –
Send me your salvation,
Which you said would come to pass;

Then I'll turn upon the taunters,
Steadfast to their jibes,
Because I trust the rock that is
Your Word, which I imbibe.

I long to taste the word of truth:
O let it fill my mouth
And take it not away,
That I may tell to north and south

How I shall always keep your laws
And in your judgement hope,
How I stand with you forever,
Never to elope.

I will walk with liberty,
No chain upon my feet
Nor rope to bind my hands
Nor any terror of defeat:

I study your commandments,
And so my soul is free
To speak before the cruellest kings
And never danger see.

I delight in your command
And will not be ashamed;
I have set my love on you,
And I will not be blamed.

~7: Zayin~

I am your servant:
Don't forget the promise that you spoke,
Your Holy Word on which alone
I've built my house of hope:

This, my only comfort
When comes sorrow like a sea,
Your promise like a lighted lamp
When darkness swallows me.

Proud people have poured scorn on me,
And cruelly they deride,
But from your law and covenant
I have not turned aside.

Yes, I have known consolation
When I think on you,
Recalling how your judgement
Lasts forever, and is true.

I burst with indignation
When I see the wicked gloat,
Who cast aside your law
And pour such evil from their throat!

My mouth brims with statutes
Which to me sound sweet as song:
   I journeyed far in pilgrimage
     To be where I belong.

Day and night I've kept your law,
   Reflecting on your name –
   I kept your commandment,
And you blest me for the same.

~8: Heth~

I've nothing but you, O God,
   My portion in this life:
   I promised to be faithful,
To refrain from worldly strife.

I beg of you, with all my heart:
   Be merciful to me,
For I have seen my wicked ways
   And turned my steps to thee.

I walk now on the righteous path –
   I did not make delay,
   But hasted to obey your laws
     And find again your way.

The wicked would entangle me,
   They wrap me in their cords,
   But I will not be tempted
To forget their true rewards.

At midnight will I rise for you,
To pour out all my thanks
Because your deeds are righteous
And most blessed are your ranks –

We are close companions,
All those who worship you,
Those who with due reverence
Keep your commandments too.

The Earth is full and brimming, Lord,
With love you have poured out;
Instruct me in your statutes
That I neither fear nor doubt!

~9: Teth~

As you said you would, Lord,
You have governed graciously –
Teach true understanding
And true knowledge, Lord, to me!

I am your humble servant,
I have done as you command –
Once I went astray before
I knew what had been planned,

But now I keep your Word
For you are full of grace and good;
For my good you afflicted me
And this I understood.

The proud have poured out vicious lies
　　To smear me with their filth,
　　But I will trust my heart to you
　　　Who lay a richer tilth.

They are grown so gross with fat
　　Because they serve themselves,
　　But I delight to serve you:
For your truth my conscience delves!

Good it is to be afflicted
　　With such woe and pain
　　That I might learn your statutes
　　And from selfishness refrain.

Some get happy from a hoard
　　Of gold and silver store,
　　But better, so much better,
　　Are the riches of your law!

~10: Yodh~

Your hands have made and fashioned me,
　　You formed me from but dust:
　　　Give me wisdom,
That in your commandments I might trust.

Those who live in awe of you
　　Shall see me and be glad:
　　All my hope has been in you
　　And in the Word you bade.

I know, Lord, your decisions
To be good and right and true;
You caused me to be troubled –
This was faithfulness from you,

Since your faithful love stayed with me,
Comforting my heart;
O Lord, do not forget your promise
Never to depart!

Let your mercy softly hold me
Yet, that I may live:
My delight is in your law,
Obedience I give.

The proud in their perversity
Accuse me with their lies –
Shame them in their falsehood,
Let my heart be sound and wise!

I meditate on your commands,
So let them come to me –
All who aren't ashamed to know
Your true testimony.

~11: Kaph~

My soul for your salvation craves
As pines a longing love;
Hoping for your Word mine eyes
Search out the sky above –

Yea, they fail with watching
While I wait impatiently,
And wail out from this bleak world,
'Lord, when will you comfort me?'

My supple skin has dried out
Like a wineskin in the smoke;
Long I wait, forgetting not
The statutes that you spoke.

How long must I go on like this?
How many are my days?
When will you requite my foes
The evil of their ways?

The proud set up a pit for me,
Defying your just law –
Help me, for with falsehood
They harangue and press me sore!

They almost made an end of me,
My wasting on this Earth,
But I held to your true commands,
Which more than life are worth!

Lord, now give me life,
For only kindly love are you,
And I shall keep your mouth's command,
Your testimony true.

~12: Lamedh~

Your Word is everlasting:
It beyond the sky stands fast,
Your faithful love and grace
Through every generation last.

You established Earth and made
It steadfast in its place:
All matter is your servant,
And you own each creature's race.

If I hadn't loved to keep your law,
I would have died
When trouble came upon me,
Yet in life I still abide.

For I do not forget your law –
By this you let me live,
I am yours alone so save me:
Your compassion give!

The wicked have long waited
To assault me in the way;
They seek to destroy me,
But to you alone I pray.

My thoughts are always on your words
For these outlast all things;
I have seen perfection rot,
The end that cruel Time brings,

But your command has conquered Time,
Your word will not be bound,
And when all things are aged away
Your faithfulness is sound.

~13: Mem~

Lord, I love your law:
My only study all day long,
To know your words, which make me wiser
Than all who do wrong.

Mine enemies are ever at my heels,
But your command
Is ever in my heart,
A certain refuge on demand.

You have made me wiser
Than the teachers and the old,
Because I contemplate your laws
And keep what I am told:

I meditate on your commands,
I strive to, night and day,
Restrain my feet from stumbling
To a broad but evil way.

Never do I turn aside,
For you have taught me well:
Your words ring from your pupil's tongue
As your sweet truth I tell.

Sweeter far than honey
Are your words upon my tongue;
Happy have I been
To know your help since I was young.

Your commands, they give me
Understanding quite complete,
And as a bitter poison
I detest all vain deceit.

~14: Nun~

Your Word is like a lantern shining,
Lightening up my path
To show the way of peace
Amidst a world of dark and wrath;

I have sworn, and will fulfil
The promise that I made
To keep the righteous judgements
And commandments that you bade.

Still, I am yet troubled,
More than measurement can mark:
I beg you, Lord, to keep your Word
And give to me life's spark.

My speech is my fine offering;
I give my praise to you –
Teach to me your judgements
That I might know what do to.

My soul rests in mine own hand;
I will not forget your law –
The wicked set a trap for me,
And yet I shall endure.

To the end I will keep
Your commandments, all my days:
It is very joy to me
To journey in your ways.

My heritage your testimony,
From the very start,
I will live your statutes out
With all my mind and heart.

~15: Samekh~

I despise the double-minded
Who pretend to pray:
My love is for your law
And those who practise what they say.

You, God, are a place for me
To hide, you are my shield;
All my hope has been in you,
The truth you have revealed.

Be gone from me, you wicked ones:
The Lord is my defence:
He promised to sustain me,
And He deals not in pretence.

I will not be disappointed
In the hope I hold –
Bear me up, O God, and save me
As you said of old!

My delight shall be in living
As you have laid out;
Those who do not go this way
Are nothing and cast out.

Vain is their deception
And their wicked gain is naught.
But as precious gold I love
The testament you've taught.

When I feel your presence, Lord,
I tremble in my awe –
I confess my terror
At the judgement yet in store.

~16: Ayin~

I have stayed true to what is just;
I have done what is right –
Do not leave me helpless
'Gainst my cruel oppressors' might!

Help your humble servant,
Bring the proud oppressors down –
Mine eyes are growing dim in watching
For your saving crown!

I wait upon your promise:
O afford to me your love –
Deal with me in kindness
As your tender-hearted dove.

Give me understanding,
Teach your servant your decrees,
And let it be that I should know
Your fair testimonies.

It is time for you to act –
They snigger at your law,
And trample your commands in ways
I utterly abhor.

Finer than great hoards of gold,
I value your command:
Let your precious precepts guide me,
Lead me by the hand,

And set upon the righteous path
Your servant's humble feet;
Deliver me from falsehood,
From the wicked one's deceit.

~17: Pe~

More wonderful than anything
Your testimonies are:
My soul is set upon them,
Gaining guidance from afar –

Your Word is like a leading light,
I open it and see,
Giving to the simple
Comprehension's liberty.

I long for your commandments
As my body yearns for breath:
To be without your gracious gaze
To me is black as death.

Turn to me and help me,
As all those who love your name –
Order every step I take,
Let evil not defame.

Let evil have no power
On my mind or soul or way;
Save me from oppressors
Who would put me as their prey.

Shine your light upon me,
Let me see your glowing face
And teach me your commandments
That I too may dwell in grace.

Mine eyes erupt with water
And my face is damp with tears
Because the wicked spurn your way
And bring such bitter years.

~18: Tsadhe~

Lord, you are most righteous,
And your words to me most true;
Everything by faithful judgement
Is arranged by you.

By mine indignation
I am wholly eaten up,
Because all these mine enemies
Your order interrupt.

Have these fools forgotten
To respect your Holy Word?
It was tried and tested,
To ignore it is absurd!

Indeed, your servant loves it,
Though I humble be, and small:
I do not neglect
To live according to your call.

Your righteousness will last forever,
Yours the timeless truth
Which has stood the test of ages,
When put to the proof.

Trouble and depression
Took me hold and pressed me down,
Yet my heart's delight remains
Your Word of such renown.

Everlasting is the righteous
Way of your command;
Grant that I your testament
May live to understand!

~19: Qoph~

God, I call upon you
From the bottom of my heart:
Answer me, that from your statutes
I may never part!

To you I call – O save me, God,
And I shall keep your law –
On your Word and testimony
I set all my store.

Early in the morning
I cry out my prayer to you,
Before the night's dark watches
I consider what is true,

Opening mine eyes that I
May meditate on this:
Hear my voice and give me, Lord,
Your life-affirming kiss.

According to your judgement,
To your faithfulness and love,
Look upon the malice
Of the wicked from above.

See, they persecute me,
In their evil spurning you,
But you, O Lord, are close at hand
And your command is true.

I have known your testimony
Long as I recall –
Your Word is a firm foundation,
Never will it fall.

~20: Resh~

Look upon my pain and torment,
Mine afflictions see –
Lord your law is always
In my mind – deliver me!

Show them that my cause is just,
Redeem me from my foe,
Let me live according
As you promised long ago.

The wicked will not find salvation,
Since they seek you not –
Your commandment they ignore,
Your worship they forgot.

Great is your compassion, God,
And you will give me life:
Though my persecutors
And oppressors may be rife,

From your righteous testament
And judgements I'll not stray;
It grieves me when I see the wicked
Scheming by the way.

The treacherous despise your Word,
The sum of which is truth;
See, Lord, how I love your Word
And make my life the proof

Of your great loving-kindness
Which will endlessly endure,
And your judgements, just and fair,
Which last forever more.

~21: Shin~

Potentates and princes
Persecute me for no cause,
Yet in awe of you my heart
Will stand; my breath takes pause:

Your Word gives me gladness,
More than one who finds great wealth;
As for lies, I hate them
And detest deceitful stealth.

Your law is my only love,
And seven times a day
To praise you and your righteous judgements
I take time to pray.

Those who love your law
Become the dwelling-place of peace;
Nothing shall perturb them,
Their blessings never cease.

I looked for your salvation
And your just commands I kept;
My soul within the boundaries
Of your testament has slept,

For greatly have I loved them,
Fulfilling all your word;
Your commandments I obeyed,
Just as I had heard.

Look upon my life, O Lord,
And see that I am true:
For all my ways and thoughts and doings,
They are plain to you.

~22: *Taw*~

Grant me understanding, Lord,
And hear my bitter cry:
Let it come before you,
And instruct me as to why

Distress has come upon me –
O help me, as you said,
And let my mouth with all your words
And statutes now be fed.

Then my lips shall pour forth praise,
My tongue sing out for you –
Of your good commandments
And the gracious deeds you do.

Stretch your hand out to me, Lord,
And help me from my plight;
I have chosen your commands
And kept them in my sight.

O, how I have longed
For your salvation, night and day;
O, how I have loved your law,
Delighted in your way!

Let my soul live on, and it
Will praise you more and more;
Let your judgements guide me
And deliver me to shore –

I have strayed far from you
Like a ship tossed on the sea,
Or a sheep that wanders lost –
O, seek and rescue me!

120

When troubles overwhelmed me,
When sorrow sapped my days,
When caught in a conspiracy –
A web of crooked ways –
I called out to God,
I poured my crying heart out loud;
He answered me from heaven's height,
And wrapped me in His shroud.

O comfort me – for lying lips
With wicked words cut hard,
Like arrows of a warrior,
And I am torn and scarred,
Buried under burning coals –
O woe, O woe is me!
That I must lodge in Mesech,
In the tents of Kedar be!

What, God, will you give or do
To that deceitful tongue?
With enemies of peace my soul
Has dwelt since I was young,
And I am spent and wearied:
Peace is long what I have sought,
But when I spoke of it,
Instead cruel war was what they wrought!

121

I lift mine eyes, and look
Upon the hills that ring me round,
Searching for deliverance,
For to me no help is found.

My help from the Lord will come,
Who crafted Earth and skies –
He who watches over you
Will never close His eyes.

He'll keep your foot from failing,
He on Israel will keep watch;
He shall not slip to slumber,
Nor shall sleep His vigil scotch.

For God himself is He
That guards your person, night and day.
His shade will keep you from the storm,
His hand will guide the way;

The Sun, he shall not strike you down,
Though harder beats his heat;
The Moon by night, she shall not make
You shiver nor retreat;

The Lord, He will protect you
From all evil in the dark;
He shall keep your soul secure
Although the road be stark:

He will guard your going out
And watch your coming in:
From this time forth for ever
Will He keep you safe from sin.

122

I was glad, beyond compare,
When they invited me:
'Let us go together now,
The Lord's great house to see!'

And now our feet are standing here,
Within these gracious gates,
Here to see Jerusalem!
My heart with rapture waits,

Beholding here the city
Built to be a place of peace:
From the weary wars and troubles
Of the world released.

Hither do the tribes ascend,
The holy tribes of God:
Israel's children, as decreed
When they from exile trod.

And Here are set the mighty thrones,
In David's judgement hall,
Where will sit the chosen twelve
To justly judge us all.

O pray, I say, that we may see
Jerusalem in peace!
For all those who love you
May prosperity increase!

May peace prevail where there was war
Of late within your walls,
A spirit of tranquillity
Within your vaunted halls!

For all my many kindred
And companions in the faith,
I pray that this most holy place
For ever may be safe:

For the sake of God's great house
That He has set in thee,
I will strive, Jerusalem,
Your champion to be!

123

Lord my God, I look to you:
My eyes to heaven rise,
As a dog before his master
Looks with eager eyes.

As a maid looks to her mistress,
Or a serf his Lord,
So we beg before you
For the mercy you afford.

Please, O God, have mercy on us:
Pardon our attempt,
For we tried to serve you
But are laden with contempt:

The proud pour down disdain on us,
The arrogant cast scorn;
Our soul is sick from their assaults,
O leave us not forlorn!

124

If the Lord had not been with us,
When the tempest rose,
If He had abandoned us,
Surrounded by our foes,
Then would they have swallowed us,
Their anger burnt us up,
Their waters overwhelmed us
And the torrent washed us up,
Our soul be swept the raging seas
And by despair be drowned,
Our bodies ripped by gnashing teeth
And none to hear the sound!

But every blessing be to God,
Who left us not their prey,
Who freed us from the fowler's snare
As birds to fly away.
Who broke our bonds asunder,
Held His people in high worth:
Our help is in the Lord
Who made the heavens and the Earth.

125

Those who trust in God
Will like the mighty mountains stand,
Which take their root for ever
And move not at man's command.

As hills about Jerusalem,
So God guards us about:
Our God, He will protect us
Evermore, without a doubt.

The cruel staff of wickedness
Will never here hold sway;
Not on the land allotted us,
Lest good men lose their way.

Do good, O Lord, to righteous ones
And people true of heart –
Not like those in crooked ways
Whom you will tear apart

And cast away with evildoers,
Who will fail and cease –
On Israel, the righteous,
Let there evermore be peace.

126

When the Lord restored us,
Then we danced in happy dreams;
Then our days were filled with laughter,
Songs poured out like streams;

Then our tongue was joyful,
And they said, 'Zion is blest' –
The Lord indeed did great things for us,
Over all the rest.

Therefore we had happiness,
Rejoiced in former days,
But now we sow in tears
Where we once would reap with praise.

Restore again our fortunes, God,
Like rain on dried-up soil;
Like rivers in the desert,
Give us good fruit for our toil.

When we go out and weep and sow
Our seed amidst despair,
Send us home with shouts of joy
For all the sheaves we bear!

127

Unless the Lord constructs the house,
The builders build in vain;
Unless the Lord keeps safe the city,
Guardsmen give no gain:
The watchman's watch is vanity,
The workman's work is nought,
For there is no strength in them
Without the Lord they sought.

Pointless is your early rising,
Toiling all the day;
Fruitless go you late to rest,
With bread your only pay,
Working hard without your God,
These worldly wares to reap:
Seek instead His help
Who blesses those He loves with sleep.

Children are His heritage,
The fruitful womb His gift:
The offspring of one's youth are like to arrows,
Sharp and swift.
Happy is the one who has
His quiver thickly stocked;
He shall not be put to shame,
Nor by his foes be mocked.

128

Blest be you who fear the Lord,
  Who walk in all His ways:
You shall eat your labour's fruit,
  Be happy all your days;

You shall have good fortune
And your spouse shall make you glad,
  Many children budding
Like fresh branches for their dad –

Thus shall one be blest
Who only Zion's God will fear;
  You will know prosperity,
  Jerusalem see clear;

On your children's children
May your eyes rest, ere you cease;
  On your days be blessing,
  And on Israel be peace.

129

'Many times they fought against me' –
Now let Israel plea –
'Many times they sought,
From my sweet youth, to harass me.

'Their onslaught may be long and hard,
Yet have they not prevailed:
They ploughed upon my back,
They scored me deep, yet they have failed.

'The righteous Lord was with me,
And He cut their cruel cords;
He sent them back in shame and loss,
And gave them their rewards:

'The enemies of Zion,
Let them wither like the grass,
Burnt brown upon the housetops –
Let them shrivel up and pass.

'Before they have the chance to grow,
Let their foul shoots be ground:
Leave nothing for the reaper,
Not a sheaf left to be bound.

'None who pass by them will say,
"God's blessing be on you,
The blessing of the Lord",
For they'll receive their rightful due.'

130

Amidst the darkest depths
Of my despair, O Lord, I lie;
Hear my supplication,
Heed my murmur as I cry.
Let your ears consider
My regret, for who could stand
If all that they had done amiss
Was punished at your hand?

Yet I know, my Lord,
That much forgiveness dwells with you:
All the world will fear you,
For your tenderness is true.
I wait for the Lord
As in a pit I'd wait for rope;
My soul waits upon Him
Since in His word lies all my hope.

My soul waits for my Lord
More than the night watch for the day,
More than those unsleeping
Long to see the Sun's first ray;
Israel, wait for God:
In Him is mercy without bound,
He will cleanse you of
Whatever sin in you is found.

131

Lord, I do not let my heart
In haughtiness abide;
I do not raise mine eyes
To self-important looks of pride.
I do not occupy my mind
With things too great for me,
With matters of much import,
For I trust myself to thee.

Instead, Lord, I have quieted
And stilled my restless soul:
As a mother's breast
Her hungry child will console,
So my soul is rested when
I find your comfort sure:
Israel, trust in God
From this time forth for ever more.

132

Lord, do not forget the hardships
David felt for you:
How he swore an oath and vowed
For ever to be true.
O mighty One of Jacob,
You he wedded like a spouse,
Saying how he would not know
The shelter of his house
Nor climb into his bed to sleep,
Allow his eyes to rest,
Nor let his eyelids slumber,
'Till he'd given you his best:
To find the Lord a dwelling-place
In stone as in his heart,
Who from your way of righteousness
Sought never to depart.

We heard of where they'd put your Arc,
Left lying in a field;
Now we fall in reverence where
Its glory is concealed:
Entering your resting place,
To see your sign of strength –
Arise, O Lord, and enter in,
Be with us now at length!
And for your servant David's sake
Turn not away your face;
Let the faithful sing with glee,
Your priests be clothed with grace.

The Lord has sworn an oath to David
He will not retract:
'To keep your fruit upon your throne
For ever, I will act –
If your children keep my ways,
The Testament I've taught,
Never will you lack a son
Upon the throne I've wrought.'

For God has chosen Zion for himself,
To habit there,
His resting place for ever
In a land He finds most fair:
'I will bless this place, with bread
Will satisfy her poor;
With salvation clothe her priests,
Rejoicing evermore.
I will keep a lantern burning,
Mine anointed's light,
And David's foes will fall in shame,
But his crown will be bright!'

133

Look, and see how unity
Is like the smoothest oil,
Good and pleasant,
Like sweet dewdrops poured upon the head;
For us to dwell together
Is a balm for every boil,
Like perfume running down
The beard of Aaron, or instead
Like dew that springs in Hermon
To flow down the parchèd hills:
For there the Lord His promise –
Everlasting life – fulfils.

134

All you servants of the Lord,
Look up now and behold:
You who stand by night
Within His gleaming house of gold,

Even in the cherished courts,
Before the House of God,
Lift your hands and praise the Lord;
In holiness be shod:

God who made both Earth and Heaven,
Everlasting Lord,
Give thee Sion's blessing
By His gracious love outpoured.

135

O praise the name of God:
Give praise, you servants of the Lord!
You who stand within
The blessed house of His reward –
Even in the courts,
The sanctuary of the same:
Praise the Lord for He is good,
Sing out His mighty name!

Let your merry music
Celebrate what He has done!
He has chosen Jacob;
Israel's children He has won
To be His own possession –
So I know the Lord is Great,
Over all the gods,
Who in His presence fall prostrate!

He does what He pleases,
Both in Heaven and in Earth,
In the depths of Ocean
And the shallow seas' bright surf,
Bringing out the clouds from far
To cover up the sky,
Striking out with lightning
As His anger passes by.

Driving rain and tearing wind
He summons from His store,
And He it was who smote down Egypt's
Firstborn sons of yore.
The firstborn of both man and beast
He gave and took away,
When they would not heed
The wondrous signs He sent that day,

Sending down on Pharaoh
All the woe that he was due,
Smiting many other kings
And lofty nations too:
Sihon, king of Ammon,
Also Bashan's ruler Og,
And all of Canaan's kingdoms,
Were left ruined and agog.

He gave their land, a heritage
For Israel His own pride;
Your name, O God, is great
And it for ever will abide!
You will be remembered,
As the generations run,
Compassionate to those who serve you:
Vindicate your sons!

The idols that the nations praise
Are mere metal stands –
Lumps of gold and silver
That were sculpted by men's hands;

They have mouths that cannot speak
And eyes that cannot see,
Ears that have no hearing
And fixed feet that cannot flee.

No breath leaves or enters
Through their lifeless lips and nose,
And all who make or worship them
Will end up just like those.
All who put their trust in useless trinkets
To be saved,
Or machines of human making,
Are to such enslaved.

But bless the Lord, O House of Israel,
Who has set you free:
Bless Him Aaron, Levi,
And all those who faithful be –
Blessed be the Lord from Zion,
Deep her praise's wells,
And blessed from Jerusalem,
The city where He dwells!

136

Give thanks to the Lord, our gracious God:
His mercy endures for ever!
The Lord of Lords and God of gods,
His mercy endures for ever.
Who by His wisdom wrought great works –
His mercy, it fails us never –
He fixed the heavens, laid out Earth:
His mercy endures for ever.

He crafted waters, set great lights –
There's none as God so clever –
The Moon and stars, to rule the night,
For His mercy endures for ever.
The Sun as sovereign of the day –
For His mercy, it fails us never –
Our God who Egypt's sons did slay,
For His mercy endures for ever.

He brought out Israel from their land –
And His great strength snapped their tether –
By His great arm and mighty hand,
For His mercy endures for ever.
He split the Red Sea into two –
Yes, He gathered the waters together –
That Israel's people might pass through,
For His mercy endures for ever.

Pharaoh's host the Red Sea stole –
For God's mercy, it fails us never –
But through the desert we came whole,
For His mercy endures for ever.
He led us through, He smote great kings
(Who thought themselves so clever)
And gave away to us their things,
For His mercy endures for ever.

Sihon, King of the Amorites –
For God's mercy, it fails us never –
And Og of Bashan, lost their fights,
For His mercy endures for ever.
Their lands a heritage became –
For His mercy, it fails us never –
And brought us safe, our foes to shame,
For His mercy endures for ever.

He remembered us, our plight –
In bitter wind and weather –
And set us in a land aright,
For His mercy endures for ever.
All His creatures He does feed –
For His mercy, it fails us never –
Give thanks to God, our strength indeed!
His mercy endures for ever.

137

By Babylon's strange waters
In our exile we sat down,
And wept when we remembered
How we lost our bright renown.

Our lyres which we'd play in Zion
With such joy and glee,
We hung them up unplayed,
In silence, by the willow tree.

There our captors called on us,
They asked us for a song –
They asked for mirth and melody,
The ones who did us wrong!

'Sing to us those happy tunes
You used to play at home.'
How now can we sing to God,
In exile curst to roam?

Jerusalem, Jerusalem,
O if I forget you,
Let my hand forget its skill,
My tongue be turned to glue!

Let it cleave within my mouth
If I do not recall;
Let me play not anything,
And sing no song at all,

If I set you not above
My highest joy in life:
Remember, Lord, this people
That have put us in such strife!

Judge this people, Edom,
And remember what they cried:
'Down with this Jerusalem –
Let not one stone abide!

'Down with this proud city –
Let us raze it to the ground!'
O wicked daughter, Babylon,
For judgement are you bound:

Doomed unto destruction,
For most glad shall be the one
Who brings retribution
For the wicked things you've done.

Who for all your did to us,
For all our stolen sons,
Dashes on the rocks to pieces
All your little ones.

138

With my heart and soul, O Lord,
I will give thanks to you;
In sight of all the gods I'll sing
The praises that are due;
I will bow towards your Temple,
Sing to your sweet name,
Because your faithful love has kept me
Safe when danger came.

You have glorified yourself,
Your Word, for all to see;
On the day I called to you,
You stooped to answer me;
You filled my soul with strength anew,
You made the shadows flee;
Even all the kings of Earth
Shall fall on bended knee.

They shall praise you, Lord and God;
Your wisdom they have heard,
They shall sing of your great glory,
Your eternal Word;
Though the Lord is high
He holds the humble in His gaze;
The proud He ponders from afar
And marks their wicked ways.

Though I walk through trouble,
Though I enter death's dark gate,
Yet you will preserve my life:
Your glory, God, is great.

You will stretch your hand to quench
The fury of my foes;
You will keep and rescue me,
Be with me in my woes;
You will make the purpose good
You had in mind for me –
Your love is forever,
You will hear your children's plea.

139

O Lord, you know me inside out,
You've searched me through and through.
You know my every sitting down
And when I rise up too.

You mark out all my journeys,
And my resting place you see;
All my secret thoughts you fathom,
Knowing more than me.

There is not a step I take,
A word upon my lips,
But you, O Lord, will know it,
For you see my strength and slips.

If I look behind me or before me,
You are there.
You lay your hand upon me,
And you lavish me with care.

Such knowledge is too wonderful –
I cannot comprehend,
Nor hope such heights of understanding
Ever to ascend.

Where, then, could I go to,
From your spirit to be split?
Or where, then, could I flee to
If your presence I would quit?

If I climb the heights to heaven,
    You are there above;
If I sleep beneath the ground
    There too I find your love.

If I take the morning's wings
    And soar into the sky,
And to the farthest outcrop
    Of the utter seas I fly,

Even there your hand shall be upon me,
    At my side:
Even there your right hand holds
    Me upright, as my guide.

If I say, 'the blackness comes
    To cover me with night!'
If the bright day ebbs away,
    And darkness swallows light,

The darkness is not dark to you:
    The night is clear as day,
Day and night are one to you
    And still you lead the way.

You yourself created
    All my innards at my start,
You knit me in my mother's womb,
    You crafted mind and heart,

And for this I thank you,
For I'm wonderfully made;
In my every atom
It's your power that's displayed.

My frame, it was not hidden
When you wove me in the Earth:
You knew me in the secret depths
And brought me up to birth.

Your eyes beheld my yet unfinished form:
You took one look;
Already all my members then
Were written in your book.

Day by day you fashioned them,
As yet they were unseen:
How deep to me your guiding words
Since then have always been!

So many are your counsels –
More in number than the sand –
I cannot hope to count them:
In your presence still I stand.

O that you would slay the wicked,
Save me from their jaws,
Send back those who thirst for blood
And tear away their claws!

With such wicked words they speak
    Against you, meaning harm;
Evil in your name they wrongly work
    To my alarm.

Surely I oppose all those
    Who work against your will,
Surely I abhor all those
    Who rise to maim and kill –

I hate them with a perfect hatred;
    Enemies of mine
Are all who through deceitful deeds
    Are enemies of thine.

Search me out and see my thoughts,
    Examine all my heart;
Erase all trace of wickedness
    And righteousness impart.

140

Lord, be my deliverance
When violence is rife,
Be to me protection
From all those who stir up strife:

Evildoers who devise
Such scandal all day long,
Whose lips are laced with poison
And whose hearts are set on wrong.

Their tongues are sharp as serpents',
They set traps upon my way,
They seek to make me stumble;
On the innocent they prey.

They set up a snare,
They sought to catch me in their cords:
Take me from their wicked hands
And from their net of swords!

I said to God, 'you are my Lord:
Please listen to my plea;
In the day of battle,
With your armour cover me.

'You are my salvation's strength –
Lord, listen to my cry;
Let not the desire of the wicked
Pass you by.

'Look upon their cruel intent,
    And prosper not their plan,
Let their own lips' evil words
    Destroy them, every man.

'See how they surround me,
    Let them not lift up their heads:
Let the darkest of the depths
    Be their eternal beds.

'Bury them with burning coals
    That rain down from above,
Cut short the prosperity
    Of those who show no love:

'Slanderers, by wickedness
    And violence made base,
Evil deeds will hunt them down
    And take them in the chase!'

I know that the Lord will rescue
    Those who are in need;
He will mete out justice
    And reward oppressors' greed –

Surely all the righteous shall give thanks, Lord,
    To your name,
Dwelling upright in your presence,
    Freed from every shame.

141

Lord, let my crying come before you;
Hear me when I call.
Quickly come to help me
When destruction's curtains fall.
Let my prayer rise to you
As incense, and suffice
The lifting of my hands
To be the evening sacrifice.

Set watch upon my words,
And set a guard upon my lips;
Let my mouth not trespass,
Keep my tongue from careless slips,
Let my heart be not ensnared
To any evil thing;
Let me not be occupied
With wickedness, nor bring

Your servant to taste pleasures
At the table of the wrong;
Never let me fall
Into the evildoers' throng.
Let righteous teachers smite me:
Let their friendly help correct;
Do not let the oil
Of unrighteousness infect

The head and heart of one
Who on your testimony feeds,
For I pray continually
Against all wicked deeds.
Let the wicked rulers
Who oppress be overthrown;
Let them taste rebuke
When they land hard on ground of stone:

Then perhaps they'll realise
The words I spoke were sweet;
Like clods beneath the plough
Let their destruction be complete.
Let their bones, unburied,
Be strewn out before the pit:
This, the hole they dug for me,
Let them fall into it!

But mine eyes will always look
To you, O Lord my God.
You are my sure refuge;
Please defend me with your rod:
Keep me from the nets of lies,
The sharp bite of the snare;
Bring me through the traps they set
To safety in your care.

142

To my God I cry aloud –
O Lord, I beg you, hear.
I tell Him of my troubles,
Make my supplication clear.

When my spirit faints
And I am weak, Lord, you are strong;
I pour out my complaint to you –
For help, O Lord, I long!

You know the way wherein I walk,
You see the snare they set,
I am left alone by all
But you will not forget:

Nobody who knows me
Do I see at my right hand,
Nobody to care for me,
No safe place left to stand,

No hiding place to flee to,
And no comfort for my soul –
And so I cry to you, O Lord,
To make my spirit whole.

Your presence is my portion
While I live, my ends in life –
You are my sure refuge
In the hardship, storm and strife.

Listen to my voice,
For they have made me very low,
They persecute and punish me,
I cannot bear their blow:

They are far too strong for me,
In prison I remain,
But when you rescue me
I will sing praises to your name.

Bring me from my dungeon,
And with thanks I will resound;
By your bounty, righteous ones
Your servant will surround!

143

O Lord, in your great faithfulness
My humble prayer hear:
Answer in your goodness
And to my request give ear.

Do not start to judge me
As your servant: I fall short,
But there is no-one living
Who sin's clutches never caught.

Mine enemy is closing in;
My life is crushed with dread,
And here I sit in darkness
Like the spirits of the dead.

My heart within is desolate,
My spirit waxes frail;
Yet I call to mind the past,
Recall again the tale

Of all the wondrous works,
The mighty deeds you wrought of old –
Now I stretch my hands to you,
I seek your hand to hold.

Like parchèd Earth deprived of water,
So I gasp for you:
Make haste, make haste to answer
For my strength is nearly through!

Do not hide your face,
For I shall slide into despair:
Down into the lightless pit,
With all the dead to share.

Send your loving-kindness
In the daybreak, as the Sun –
In you alone I trust
And to your loving arms I run.

Show the way that I should walk:
I lift to you my soul,
I flee to you for refuge
From the wicked on patrol.

Let your spirit lead me
On the straight and level path;
Teach to me what pleases you
And guide me by your staff.

For your holy name alone,
Revive me from my woes;
Bring me safe from trouble
And destroy those wicked foes:

Slay those great adversaries,
For your great goodness' sake,
For I, Lord, am your servant
And in this there's no mistake.

144

Blessed be the Lord,
Who is the rock on which I stand,
The fortress built around me
And the strength of my right hand.
He trained my fingers for the battle,
Placed in them His shield,
Subduing all the peoples with
His mighty sword I wield.

You, O Lord, delivered me,
My stronghold and high tower:
What are we, mere mortals,
That you mark our fleeting hour?
We come and go like breaths of wind,
We bloom but once and die;
Our days pass like a shadow
When the sun ascends the sky.

Bow your heavens, break upon us,
Make the mountains smoke,
Cast down your swift arrows
That the wicked mouths may choke;
Smash the sky with lightning,
Let your thunderous anger roar;
Reach down, God, and save me
From the adversary's claw.

From the hand of falsehood fetch me,
From the water's swell –
I will now a new song sing
And of your wonders tell!
You delivered David,
Gave salvation to great kings;
From the sword that threatens me
Your shield my rescue brings.

The foreign foes may scoff at me,
Stretch forth their fingers false,
But none of their devisings may
Your mighty strength repulse.
Our sons in youth will flourish like
The best-attended trees,
Our daughters in their beauty be
Like pillars shaped to please;

Our barns be filled to bursting
With all manner of good store,
Our flocks fill fields, a thousand
Or ten thousand strong and more;
Our cattle with their young be heavy
And give healthy birth,
Our streets be clean of crying in distress,
Bedecked by mirth.

Happy are our people, Lord,
Whom you saw fit to bless;
Happy are the people who
Your mighty name confess!

145

I will exalt you, O my Lord,
O my God and King;
Throughout all eternity
Of your name I shall sing.

Every day I live I shall
Bring blessings to your name;
Ever and forever shall
My lips sing out your fame!

Your exceeding greatness
Is beyond all searching out,
Great you are and worthy
Of all praise without a doubt.

Every generation to the next
Will tell your praise,
All your works and mighty deeds,
The wonder of your ways –

They shall speak of glory,
Of your marvelled majesty;
I will tell of all the
Splendid acts you've shown to me;

They shall speak of wonders,
Of power and of might;
I will tell of all your greatness
Shown before my sight.

They shall brim with stories
As the water is poured forth,
Full of joy recounting
Your great righteousness and worth.

Our God is gracious
And His goodness is so great;
Our God is merciful,
And for His own will wait;

Our God is full of love
For every one He's made,
His mercy covers all His creatures –
Never will it fade!

All your works of majesty
Sing praise, O God, to you;
All your servants who have speech
Sing blessings to you too.

They recall your mighty power,
Your rule they reveal;
They make known to all the nations
That your strength is real;

The glory of your acts
And your great kingdom do they show;
Your dominion lasts throughout all ages –
This we know.

Your rule everlasting,
And your words for ever sure,
Your faithfulness unbreakable,
Compassionate your law!

Those who fall the Lord upholds,
The burdened He lifts high;
The eyes of all your servants wait
And watch as you pass by –

You feed them in their season,
For you open wide your hand
And every living thing is nourished
Well by your command.

Righteousness defines your ways,
Your works are only love;
God is near to those who call Him,
Under and above:

All who lift their hands to Him
In faith He gently holds;
All who cry to Him He saves
And every hurt resolves:

He fulfils the heart's desire
Of those who ask of Him;
He takes care of those who love Him –
With His grace they brim.

But the wicked He stamps out:
My mouth shouts out His praise;
Let all flesh for ever
Blessings to His great name raise!

146

Praise the Lord, my soul: O praise Him
While you yet have breath;
While I have my being will I praise Him
All my days.
Put no trust in human powers,
In princes who see death,
In the child of man
Who cannot help you, since he strays

Back into the dust of Earth,
When all his breaths are done,
And his many thoughts and fancies
Perish in a jot.
But happy he who trusts
The God of Jacob and his sons,
Which made the Earth and stars and heavens,
Oversees the lot,

And knows all truth eternally,
And executes just laws:
Who feeds the hungry, comforts
All those wrongfully oppressed,
Who looses those imprisoned,
Tossing down the bolted doors,
Who raises those bowed down by woe
And gives the weary rest.

Have your hope in God,
For He will give your blind eyes sight;
Know how much He loves His children,
All who righteous be;
The wicked He uproots,
Orphans and widows He sets right:
O Zion, praise the Lord
Whose reign you shall for ever see!

147

Alleluia! Good it is
To honour God with praise;
To make for Him sweet music
Gives us joy throughout our days.

The Lord restores Jerusalem,
Her outcasts gathers in;
He heals the woes of wounded hearts,
Salvation swaps for sin.

He counts the number of the stars,
He knows them each by name;
His wisdom is beyond all words,
His might and strength the same.

The Lord lifts up the burdened poor
And draws them from the dust,
But throws the wicked from their pride
And grounds them in disgust.

Sing to Him with thanks
And make sweet music on the lyre;
He it is who clothes the heavens,
Sets what will transpire;

Sends the rain to water grasses
High upon the hills;
Makes green plants to grow
With which His animals He fills –

He gives the beasts their food,
He hears the birdlings when they cry;
He needs not strength of horses,
Man's machines He passes by.

He delights in those who fear Him,
Trusting in His love –
Not in those who vainly boast
But spurn their Lord above.

Praise Him, O Jerusalem,
And Zion, sing His praise –
Better than your bars and gates
Is God's protecting gaze.

He it is who blest your children,
Bordered you with peace,
And gave the finest wheat to fill you
That you might increase.

When He sends forth His command,
So swiftly does it run –
He only needs to say the word
And what He wants is done.

He sends the snow, a woollen sheet,
The frost as scattered ash,
He rains down hail like bits of bread;
To risk His ire is rash.

He sends the word and melts the frost,
Dissolves away the snow;
He wields the wind to dry the flood
And lets the waters flow.

He speaks His word to Jacob
And lets Israel know His law,
His statues and His judgements,
Like no nation has before.

148

Alleluia! Praise the Lord:
Praise Him from the heights!
Praise Him from the heavens' heavens,
All you shining lights!
Praise Him, all you angels,
Praise Him all His mighty host;
Praise Him Sun and Moon and stars,
And of his glory boast!

Praise Him swirling waters
That above the deep skies flow;
Let them praise the Lord,
All He created here below.
At His word they took their being,
By His skill set fast:
He decreed the laws of nature
That shall never pass.

Praise Him from the deepest depths,
All sea monsters beneath;
Praise Him, all the Earth,
The elements He did bequeath:
Fire, snow, hail and mist
That tumble from His hand,
And the wind and tempest
That blow forth at His command.

Mighty mountains, hallowed hills,
All woods and fruiting trees,
Wild beasts and cattle,
Creeping things, all birds and bees,
Kings of Earth and all its peoples,
Princes, all who rule,
Young and old, both men and women,
Counted wise or fool –

All together praise the Lord,
Let all creation sing,
For His name alone in splendour
Over all we bring,
Exalted to the heavens,
For He raised His people's horn
And brought His servants mercy –
We, the seed to Israel born!

149

Alleluia! To the Lord
Now sing a novel song:
Where the faithful gather,
Sing his praise, you cheerful throng!

In their mighty maker
Now may Israel rejoice:
To their righteous king
Let Zion's children lift their voice!

Let them play with timbrels,
Let them praise Him as they dance;
Let them joy in glory,
Gird with gladness their great ranks!

For the Lord takes pleasure
In the people that He chose;
He adorns the poor and humble
With salvation's rose.

The people praise their God
With gracious words upon their lips,
And a two-edged sword
Each faithful warrior now grips

To bring down God's swift vengeance
On the nations of the Earth,
To punish all the peoples
Who have proven little worth.

God will bind the kings in chains,
Who mocked Him in their pride;
Nobles, clapped with iron fetters,
In disgrace abide:

This will be the judgement
The Almighty One decreed,
And honoured are the faithful servants
Sent to do this deed.

150

Alleluia! Praise the Lord:
Praise our Holy God!
Praise Him in the essence
Of His power, strong and firm!
Praise Him for His greatness,
For the mighty steps he trod;
Praise Him for His awesome acts,
For which we have no term:

Praise instead with blasting trumpet,
Praise with harp and lyre!
Praise and play and dance and sing
Upon the strings and pipe!
Let the mighty symbols clash,
Let praises roar like fire!
Let everything with breath break forth
With praises, sweet and ripe!

www.ingramcontent.com/pod-product-compliance
Lightning Source LLC
Chambersburg PA
CBHW070418010526
44118CB00014B/1801